The Blessedness of *Brokenness*

FRANK SHELTON, JR.

Copyright © 2012 by Franklin Shelton, Jr.

ISBN: 978-0-578-10064-7

ETERNITY
P.O. Box 742
Waldorf MD 20604

Printed in the United States of America

Contents

FOREWORD

"IF there is one thing I have learned in the ministry, it is that we serve a God of second chances. I have seen countless lives transformed from brokenness to a thriving existence full of hope and determination. Far too often the body of Christ will give up on people, when they are only a few compliments and encouragement away from a breakthrough. The Bible is full of flawed people who found a calling on their life and ended up being some of the greatest servants of the Lord. Love is the most revolutionary force in this world, a force that can rebuild lives, renew hope, and strengthen the community. We are called to be representatives of Christ's love. It is the greatest gift that anyone could ever have. The truth is that you will never really know someone's potential until you give them a chance. I believe that the church should be a hospital for the broken people of the world, and not a waiting room for the saints.

At the Dream Center, I am constantly amazed by the lives that are transformed into ones of purpose and confidence. In our recovery program, we have every type of story from ex-gang members, former prostitutes, and recovering drug addicts who discovered God's love and found brand new purpose. Many of our volunteers felt like they had nothing left in their lives, until they understood God's grace and found renewed belief in their future. They discover the joy of serving others on our food outreach sites and cleaning up the community, and they find a bond in their brothers and sisters who have seen similar hard times. Where once not long ago was a gang member who might bring fear to others, is a radiant vessel of hope with a huge smile on their face. Everyone should feel accepted in the house of the Lord. For we all fall short of God's glory, and this is what makes us human. It is the acceptance of that humanity, and loving one another unconditionally that should be the aim of the church. I believe in broken people. *Often times I find that those who felt like they had nothing to give, end up giving the most*. It is not our duty to judge others, but to believe in them and see the amazing possibilities which come from a second chance."

Pastor Matthew Barnett
Co-Founder of **The Dream Center**
Author of NY Times Best Selling Book
"The Cause Within You"
Los Angeles, California

"As surprising as it first seemed, in time Apostle Paul discovered that he was much more fruitful with thorns and afflictions than he was without them. The *discomfort* of his *predicament* wasn't nearly so bad once he saw the *design* of God's *purpose*.

Apart from that divine revelation, troubles and heartaches are generally seen as something ugly and foreboding - a frightening and terrifying enemy to hurt and to harm us. And yet, for the maturing believer, many times these thorns are given for good. He touches us with affliction that He may teach us His affection. That's why Paul could so confidently declare, "*...Most gladly therefore will I rather glory in my infirmities that the power of Christ may rest upon me* (II Corinthians 12:9)."

Junior Hill
Evangelist & former **VP of Southern Baptist Convention**
Hartselle, Alabama

"Brokenness has been part of the DNA of the human race since the fall of man. The plain and simple fact is that in one way or another we are all broken. The good news, however, is that God is not waiting until we are healed or feel whole before using us for His noble tasks. Thankfully, fulfilling His purpose for our lives is not entirely dependent upon us. Most of it is based on His grace, which allows us to accomplish incredible things in spite of ourselves and regardless of our past or present circumstances. Unfortunately, many of us count ourselves out of the race or discount our potential simply because we are flawed or broken. The greatest tactic of the enemy is to get you to focus on your flaws rather than on the God who is able to bring blessedness through that brokenness. Regretfully, we learn to magnify our weaknesses instead of magnifying God who makes His people strong amidst their weakness by learning to rely on Him. The great French novelist Victor Hugo asserted, "Have courage for the great sorrows of life and patience for the small ones; and when you have laboriously accomplished your daily task, go to sleep in peace. God is awake." Yes, indeed, God is awake and more than capable of turning our tragedies into triumphs and our mourning into dancing.

Until we are truly broken, most of us are fairly self-centered and lack the genuine compassion necessary to truly care for others. The true power and effectiveness of our personal ministry will always be birthed from our points of pain, and it is precisely this necessary suffering which helps us develop a heart to serve. Helen Keller reflected, "Character cannot be developed in ease and quiet. Only through experience of trial and suffering can the soul be strengthened, ambition inspired, and success achieved." We all cherish times of prosperity, but we really only grow in times of great pressure and pain. Then, out of that brokenness comes forth the true gold.

My brokenness is nothing compared to the magnitude faced by many people written about in this book. My inner pain and turmoil were real to me though, and I struggled for most of my life with the brokenness that comes from being abandoned by your father. Rejection, low self-esteem and self-loathing are all part of the emotional fallout and among the many obstacles that can only be overcome by receiving God's love. I eventually learned that we do not have to earn His love. He just loves us because we are His children, and He loves us unconditionally.

Once I grasped that revelation, it was like being handed a "get out of jail free" card. It removed the two-ton emotional boulder off my back, which I had been carrying around since childhood. Additionally, it was through brokenness that my father heart was born. After being a Godly husband, being a father to my children has always been my No. 1 priority as a man. It is one of the greatest joys of my life. Through God's grace, I also developed a father's heart for a fatherless generation. I became for many others what I always longed for myself – encourager.

I know another man who is an encourager, who also possesses the same father's heart and relentless passion for doing good. A man who poured his heart and soul into this book to help launch you into the destiny God has for you. He is Frank Shelton, a man about his Father's business and a man whom I have the privilege to call a friend. Frank is a one-of-a-kind individual who possesses a rare combination of depth and tenacity coupled with a great sense of humor and genuine love for others. He is an authentic man and one who has discovered the lost art of living for a purpose. His is to encourage you to trust that God can still do great and mighty things through you, no matter how broken you may be or how useless, inadequate or unqualified you may feel.

He is correct, because with God all things are possible. In 2 Chronicles 16:9, scripture says, "The eyes of the Lord search the whole earth in order to strengthen those whose hearts are fully committed to him." God only needs a willing vessel to display His power, love and greatness; the great news is that you can be the vessel! I implore you to commit your heart fully to Him today and watch the Lord do miraculous things through you, making a difference in your lifetime and having a rippling effect throughout all of eternity. I am decreeing now at the moment of your reading this book that a season of blessedness will find its way to you!"

Zoro, The Drummer
"The Minister of Grove"
Nashville, Tennessee

Zoro is a world-renowned drummer who has toured and recorded with Grammy Winners Lenny Kravitz, Frankie Valli & The Four Seasons, New Edition, Bobby Brown, Tom Petty, Lisa Marie Presley, Sean Lennon & many more! Zoro & Frank Shelton are both Compassion International speakers/sponsors and flew to Guatemala together to help rescue children from poverty in Jesus name. Zoro, is also an "in demand" speaker and author of the critically acclaimed book, "The Big Gig: Big-Picture Thinking For Success." www.zorothedrummer.com, www.zoromin, istries.org, www.thebiggigbook.com

"SPECIAL DELIVERY"

IN 1992, (age 20) I preached a sermon that God gave me called "*The Blessedness of Brokenness.*" Since grade school I loved to play with words and live today to allow the Word to have His way with me. At the time, I had never heard of anyone putting the two words *broken* and *blessing* together. Many in our society would think they are an oxymoron.

Interesting enough on the title the Lord gave me the text and an outline to share how He uses the dark, dry seasons in our life to draw us closer to Him and bless others in the process. Many were touched because of the Truth resting on that message and I am convinced it is inspired and breathed on by Almighty God. Not long after preaching that sermon I gave the message on cassette to my dear friend and now pastor, Rev. Marvin Harris (also an author in this book). He told me later that he loved the message after listening but laughed initially thinking "*What does this kid know about being broken?*"

Some call it prophetic and a few even pathetic but I knew that I was on to something. As I write this I am on the doorstep of reaching a birthday milestone. On February 20, 2012, Lord willing, I will turn 40 and truth be told I am surprised that I'm still here. I never dreamt I would still be around. Why? Early in life, I thought two things. Either, I am on my way out or God is on His way back. Personally, ministry without urgency leads to *catastrophe*. Jesus repeated "Today's the day of Salvation." Billy Graham called it the "Hour of Decision."

Similar to a woman knowing daily that her biological clock was ticking I always felt since childhood my window to touch the world for God's glory was closing sooner rather than later. Without question, I am not the sharpest tool in the shed and never once the smartest kid on the block but God has granted me more than my share of wisdom. Like a blind man who has a tendency to pick up on or even "see" things that most folks with vision overlook God has allowed me to witness remarkable truths that I have been dying to share.

This book has been brewing in me for sometime and I wanted to pour it out in life before it evaporated in my death. My first book that I wrote "FINAL APPROACH – Career vs Calling?" was unique in that I wrote it in a mere five days. That is not a typo and it was as if I was reading it as I wrote it. This book was different. Actually, much different! The fact is this book was birthed in me first but I didn't have the green light from God to deliver it. The average pregnancy lasts nine months. Today, you hold in your hands the baby (message) that God entrusted to me over two decades ago.

We all have heard stories of premature babies but very few are familiar with child bearing long overdue. This book could have been delivered sooner but was hindered for various reasons. Complications come at a moment's notice and I had certainly lived long enough to share credibly the insights God gave me and tested them to be true but still wasn't released to release it. Perhaps one reason for the delay was that the audience (you) may have not been ready to receive the message birthed until now. Secondly, while crisscrossing the Country I have been blessed to connect with all of the authors in this book and growing as friends with them and hearing their remarkable stories made the wait worthwhile.

Its not that I wasn't ready but the book maturing in me wasn't ready. We find wisdom in waiting because if we are not still with God we may have a stillborn on our own. The book (baby) is not just mine but theirs and yours as well. Here is a snapshot of the heartbeat of this book. Since a child, God revealed me a truth that many are now just discovering. This will be a game changer for some and a life changer for others. Get ready, sit down, buckle up, get your helmet on, drum roll please......

God doesn't just use the "blessed" but *broken* people the most.

The Lord allowed me to *SEE* that those whom endured the most usually were used the most for His glory. When I mention "used" it is in a positive way. In the world being "used" is negative and you feel like trash. When the Lord "uses" you it is not trash but a treasure and highest honor in life. We live in a society that suggests if you are *bruised, broken* or *battered* you are trash and discarded. Well, I got GOOD NEWS for you! It is true that one man's junk is another Man's treasure. Yes, I am talking that Divinity delights, Lord loves and God gravitates towards those that have been through some storms.

Jesus fed five thousand and on another occasion He fed four thousand. One afternoon while Jesus was en route to Jericho, He walked up to Zacchaeus in a tree. The little guy was out on a limb to the see Lord. He was not only short in stature, sophisticated in sinning but now a *sicko* in the Sycamore. This tax collector his entire life knew what it was like to be on the "outside looking in." With the Lord, you never know what you're going to get. God could have fed the multitudes again but on that night he elected to have dinner for two.

The Trinity is now at the base of the tree and the Lord looked, laughed and listened. God rather be a personal Savior than a professional and as always with God in the picture He changed every thing (for our good). Politicians tend to leave individuals to cater to crowds but Christ left crowds to bless an individual. Like the Good Shepherd whom left the 99 sheep to go save one the Lord lived that passage here while connecting with Zacchaeus.

Jesus knew beforehand that Zacchaeus had money in the bank but no Savior in his tank. He was fixed financially but bankrupt spiritually and while the world looks at the outward appearance God gazes at the heart and elected to go to his home. The world longs for *food, fellowship* and *forgiveness* and God as the Trinity is not only "three in one" but could provide all three at once. The guy (Zacchaeus) whom spent his whole life on the outside looking in as a rejected, broken businessman is now for the first time in his life on the inside looking out conversing with God on a dinner date.

This was the night that God gave this guy grace as Zacchaeus the *sinner* met Jesus the *Winner* and together they went out for *dinner*! That was the first ever "Happy Meal." It was a candle light dinner for two because when the Light of the World is dining at your table His light burns bright not only in our hearts but our homes. The Bible doesn't reveal what they ate but after finding a feasting in fasting I firmly believe I know what they had the day the *sinner* had *supper* with the *Savior*. Get ready – **The Lord loves** *leftovers*! When the world walked out is when the Word Himself walks in. Even when Jesus fed five thousand He told His disciples "gather the remaining bread (leftovers) *that nothing* (or no one) be lost." Jesus came to seek and save that which was lost.

Misfits, rejects and leftovers are not on man's radar but they are on the Redeemer's. They show up instantly on the Savior's screen and Christ chases the crooked and crusty.

Leadership courses teach that leaders should intentionally distance themselves from certain people. Lordship doesn't distance but dies for those same castaways. Computers have screen savers but Christians' have a slain Savior. God doesn't protect us from scars or storms but He gives peace and protection by His Presence and Promises in the process. No one likes to be picked last, over looked or worse treated as if one doesn't exist but God's heart beats for the battered and broken.

The people I admire the most often have endured the most. Without a test we wouldn't have a TESTimony. Regardless, if it were one of my heroes, Dr David Ring born with Cerebral Palsy who his own pastor told him starting out in ministry "*God cannot use you David – you have Cerebral Palsy*." David may have Cerebral Palsy but Cerebral Palsy didn't have him! David's preacher was dead wrong and 39 years later in fulltime ministry, David has now spoken in 6,000 churches and seen countless souls experience eternal life in Christ and booked nearly two years in advance. His own pastor told him "no" but God said "yes!"

One of America's national treasures and my mentor, Evangelist Tim Lee lost both legs in the Vietnam War after stepping on a land mine fighting for freedom was told by many ministers and church leaders: "*Brother Tim, God cannot use you – you are in a wheel chair*." At least Brother Tim was in the WILL of God. Some "clowns" tried to give him the red light but God granted green to roll on for the Redeemer. Praise God that Tim didn't stop after hearing the reckless rhetoric of the religious but adhered to the still, small voice of the Almighty. Today, Tim has preached around the globe in some of the largest arenas and held audiences with U.S. Presidents, Dr Billy Graham, world-class athletes and countless crowds. Just last month, Tim returned from preaching to the masses in India. The horrible grenades of these callous claims were arguably more harmful than the devastation of disease and/or war.

Never let the reckless rhetoric of the religious or irrelevant hinder you from your dinner date or destiny with Divinity.

I'm mindful of my buddy, Josh Shipp who I had the pleasure to fly to California and officiate his wedding. Josh and I co-authored a book in 2000, called "The Best of Teen Success" with our friend, Sam Glenn. Josh was orphaned at the hospital and never met his parents and today known across America on his hit show "JUMP SHIPP" on Halogen TV and just named 30 under 30 in INC. magazine plus the highest paid youth speaker in history. Years ago, I coined a phrase that those whom travel the furthest tend to go the farthest. One of my dear friends is Tony Nolan whom had a less than stellar upbringing in Florida and yet God used him tremendously the past six years as tour pastor of Winter Jam to reach and rescue nearly half a million souls for salvation in Jesus. My college buddy, Clayton King was born out of wedlock to a single mother and praise God didn't abort him and now the campus pastor at Liberty University seeing countless lives changed weekly.

My friend, Tammy Trent lost her husband ten years ago while drowning on a missions trip and today she speaks and sings to hundreds of thousands of people annually with the life changing message of Jesus, The Christ at Women of Faith Conferences and world-wide television. My dear friend and Grammy Winner Michael English has had mountain top successes and deep, dark valleys but very few are used more of God today in Christian music circles. Two months ago, I finally got to meet one of my heroes,

Nick Vujicic. That brother from another mother was born with no limbs but he also knows NO LIMITS! How could a man with no arms or feet be used? With men it may be impossible but with God ALL things are possible. Mark Hall – front man to Grammy Winner *Casting Crowns* has A.D.D. and yet has penned some of the greatest praise songs of our generation and they've been named "Group of the Year" the past four years! Go God!! Rick Heil – lead singer to SONICFLOOd is a dear friend and he almost died with Chron's Disease.

Those that really have something to pout about with God in the equation have something to SHOUT! One of my best friends, Michael Cramer's dream was to become a special agent. For nearly a decade he was with the U.S. Capitol Police on their Dignitary Protection Detail and he guarded Members of Congress and world leaders. Mike is a sold out Christian and in his late 30's he learned that his ribs were pushing down on his chest towards his heart and it could kill him. He had an emergency surgery and the physicians made a mistake during the operation and after a painful nine month recovery had to cut him open again. The police department has a policy that you cannot be out for more than one consecutive calendar year and because of another's mistake he was forced to retire prematurely from his dream job. God had a plan all along and now Mike has an amazing ministry with motorcycle bikers and active in prison ministry across America and has personally led scores to salvation in Christ in various states and countries. He went from protecting earthly kings to promoting The King of kings. The blessing is Mike was honoring God in both situations by his life and lips. **The Redeemer relishes in resurrections!** What looked like the end was just a transition and page turned in the next chapter of Michael's life.

The list is almost endless but I am also reminded of my dear friend, Basketball Hall of Fame and fellow evangelist Meadowlark Lemon. He faced intense racial criticism while playing for the legendary Harlem Globetrotters and was good enough to dazzle tens of thousands nightly but during the Civil Rights era many esteemed not worthy enough to dine in certain restaurants because of his skin color. He could have got bitter but he chose to become better and the rest is history and we are all blessed for it. His pain in private became millions of fans JOY in public and regardless if playing to sold out crowds at Madison Square Garden, dining with the First Lady at the White House, having tea with the Queen of England, befriending the poor or spending time at the Martin Luther King Memorial in Washington, DC with me fifty years later God truly uses our hurts to help others. How can this be? I have found "blessedness in brokenness" and you can too!

The beauty about being broken is you don't need to be famous but you must know firsthand that He is faithful. Lean into Him during your weak moments and together you will tap into strength like you've never known. One of my favorite verses of Scripture is 1 Corinthians 1:27 *"God uses the foolish to confound the wise."* Ironically, I have always substituted foolish for "broken" or imperfect. The fact is all of us are broken (even the one's casting clueless stones). Pharisees may have no room for us but take heart they didn't have room for Jesus either. Religion is a dead end but my Redeemer turns dead ends into launching pads for life and victorious living! When others say you can't do it they are just telling on themselves that "no" they can't but you and I can still do ALL things with God who strengthens us. The next time someone looks down on you remember to smile, shake the dust off your feet like Christ and look up in worship and move on!

Use their rocks to build a staircase to climb higher in the call Christ compelled you from the beginning. One lie that Satan has used and too many have believed for centuries is that for us to be used of God either must be perfect or encountered little hardship. Fact number one, NO ONE except Christ is perfect. Secondly, the folks that I admire and appreciate the most are usually the very ones whom have endured the most. Many see us on stage publicly but they don't see the stain privately. They may mistake some for "stars" but failed to realize it's our *scars* that are most valuable.

Adversity is preparing you for God's varsity. God may love us the same but He doesn't use us all the same. At times, I felt like a rubber band with the stress and strain in my life pulling me backwards and I honestly thought *"Lord, if I get stretched another inch I will snap."* The blessing is God is not snapping us but SHAPING us to resemble Him. The resistance in your life now will determine the distance you will travel later.

While a guest on "ATLANTA LIVE" interviewed by Shelley Hendrix on television while sitting on their Oprah-like couch that I shared a story of a college football running back that broke his forearm in multiple places. He went to doctor after doctor only to hear repeatedly that "because of that break – your career on the football field is over." It crushed him and with one last doctor visit reaching out to hope he came across a Christian physician that told him "Yes, it is bad but I have good news. I have come to the conclusion that if you allow me to touch it and heal it over time it is a medical fact that the bone becomes stronger AFTER the break than before! If that doesn't light your fire than your wood is wet!

It has been eloquently said: "Adversity causes some men to break and others to break records." Which one are you? Today is a new day!

From this point forward see stress as a friend not your enemy. Your mess today may become your MESSage tomorrow. Your hurt now when given to God will bring hope and healing to countless hurting people. Your near death tragedy will bring new life experiences to all if you just give it to God, hold on and praise Him in your storms.

Oswald Chambers said: "The storms you encounter were never really meant for you. It was that you could relate to others in their moment of pain and that is where your ministry begins." Ministry often starts at a moment of pain. Even Jesus when He left Divinity to be dipped in humanity was birthed in a barn of Bethlehem. Not glorious but the Gospel Truth. At birth, Mary was crying and Jesus was *dying* to get out. As Jesus, the kid whom was already King rolled out of the crib He was immediately en route to our cross. Your pain will become another's promotion later. God never wastes a trial and He won't waste yours!

What was almost your end is another's beginning. I have found an anointing on folks who have been tested. Grammy Winner Mark Lowry of the Gaither Vocal Band was right when he said: "*God uses broken pots most because they leak more water.*" Your cracks are a temporary crisis today but when given to Christ our creator He will use you for His glory in a future tomorrow. God never sees souls as trash. Actually, He treasures them.

Man discards but the Messiah delivers. People can relate to authenticity and are hungry for genuine ministry. Stained glass windows are beautiful. Many think it's because of their colors but actually it's the cracks in the panes that make them colorful and valuable. When the light shines through the cracks the colors EXPLODE! When Jesus, The Light of the world shines powerfully through our stains, storms and scars an anointing automatically oozes out of us and brings glory to God and hope and healing to hurting people.

If Jesus wasn't a carpenter I believe He would be in the automobile body and fender business. Why? God loves and lives to restore old, broken down and damaged goods. God in His grace picks us up, dusts us off and whispers affirmation in our ears and sends us out to change the world. Broken people can *relate*. Broken people *reveal* His grace. Broken people are *ready* to get things done. Broken people are willing to *roll* while pious punks are sitting stagnant on the sofa. Here is something to soak in –

Rejects once inspected are expected to do great things.

Nearly 25 years ago, I was told by a preacher: "Preach to the broken hearted because there is one in every pew." He was part right. Over the years, I have found a broken heart in almost every chair. Indeed, I have found a blessing in being broken and the next time you are sitting out in an audience and see someone on stage it's not because they are better but they didn't get bitter. It's not that they deserve it but God reserved that slot for them. Your disappointments today are Divine appointments tomorrow.

As you read this book take an inventory of your life and my prayer for you is that these stories give you renewed hope to be all you are created to be for Christ. Don't be ashamed of your scars. When you stand before Jesus and He stretches out His hands towards you it is a fact that His massive palms of peace and arms of grace will still adorn scars. At one time I was impressed by His success but today I am grateful for His scars. His temporal setbacks bought my eternal salvation.

It has been said: "*A leader is not worth following who doesn't have their share of scars.*" Jesus has His and if you are honest with yourself you have yours. We don't have to hide anymore. You are a candidate to be used when you give God your broken pieces. I have shared with folks around the globe that you may be *down, discouraged, depressed*, have *debt, divorced* or *diseased* but if you are not *dead* than God is NOT done with you!"

The world's most beloved evangelist, Dr Billy Graham even knew firsthand the pain but power of being broken. His first fiancé broke up with him because she told him she wanted to marry a man who would truly make a mark in the ministry. Wow! She sure failed on that one but that setback was setting up God to work a great character building injection into what would become arguably the greatest Christian since the Apostle Paul. Plus, Billy would have missed out on the love of his life, Ruth.

Before honor comes humility. It's true the greater the break initially the bigger the blessing of possibilities. Abraham Lincoln lost fourteen elections before becoming the most quoted man in American history and reaching the Presidency. James Earl Jones was a stutter in grade school. He was mocked by his peers but today the most recognized voice in the world. His voice gave life to Darth Vader and now known around the globe for announcing "This is CNN." Michael Jordan was cut from his high school basketball team in Wilmington, NC at Langley High before graduating to win gold on the "Dream Team" in the Olympics, winning six NBA championships and selling over a billion dollars in sales with Nike's "Air Jordan." Before Jordan took flight he cried in the night after that first painful rejection. Before he learned to dunk he was blocked by his high school coach. Never let the opinion of one person hinder you from your divine destiny.

Grammy Winner Nicole C Mullen sings "Redeemer" was a guest on my radio show and she shared in the past that her first husband physically abused her. Sadly, she was hit before but today hits notes that very few on planet earth can belt out. Those that have been hit low tend to soar high. It was an honor as a child to meet briefly Olympic gold medalist and six time world champion boxing great, Sugar Ray Leonard. Ray is a Maryland native and in his new book "The Big Fight" talks about the pain of being molested as a child. Today, he is considered *"pound for pound"* one of the best boxers to ever enter the ring. Instead of fighting outside on the streets and getting in trouble with the law he adorned gloves and fought his way to the top. Plus, his bouts with Hagler, Hearns and Duran were viewed at first as opponents and obstacles but today proved to be opportunities for him to grow as a person and parent. Even the champ had his share of loses and it was after receiving the detached retina in the ring to his eye that he re-attached his priorities in life.

It was my privilege to be an "extra" for four days in Las Vegas filming "Rocky Balboa" starring Sylvester Stallone. The poetic punch of the movie came when Sly said to his son: *"It ain't about hard you can hit but how hard you can take a hit and keep moving forward."* Mark this down. **Those that have survived the deepest depression later make lasting impressions.** What do these successful people have in common? The theme of being *broken* is the common denominator.

Make no mistake this book isn't advocating fame but encouraging all to develop faith in Christ. One of the greatest honors of my life is to meet so many precious people on this road called life. Many of the authors who contributed to this baby (book) are my heroes and it's always humbling and exhilarating when we graduate from fans to friends. Today, I am still their biggest fan and I pray that our stories will bless you to love God deeper and may we reach out to others wider in service to our Lord. In this book, you are about to experience emotions that will have you laughing one minute and crying the next. From tragedy to triumph becoming trophies of grace may their testimonies inspire you to live with passion and purpose today and all your future tomorrow's.

It has been said "the only person God cannot use is the individual full of themselves." Brokenness is a great avenue to become in a better position to serve the Lord. It's worth repeating that the next time you feel like God can't use you remember Noah was a drunk, Abraham was too old, Isaac was a daydreamer, Jacob was a liar, Leah was one of the "Lee" sisters: She was *homely, smelly* and *ugly*! Joseph was abused and accused, Moses had a stuttering problem, Gideon was afraid, Samson had long hair and was a womanizer. Rahab needed rehab because she was a prostitute, Jeremiah and Timothy were "too young," David was an adulterer and a murderer, Elijah was suicidal and Isaiah preached naked (his sermon was "The Bare Facts)." Jonah ran from God and most thought "washed up" after his encounter with a whale. Naomi was a widow but God saw the window to use her! Job went bankrupt while John the Baptist ate bugs. Worse, Peter denied Christ and the disciples "fell asleep on the job" with Jesus while praying. Martha worried about everything and the Samaritan woman was divorced (more than once). Zaccheus was too small, Paul was too religious, Timothy had an ulcer and watch this - **Lazarus was dead!**

God delights in deadbeats. He loves to bless the broken, honor the hurting, fellowship with the forgotten and those whom once were burdened become blessed when touched by The Best. Jesus didn't come for the healthy (pious) but broken and sick. *"It is no secret what God can do. What He's done for others. He will do for you. With arms wide opened – He'll pardon you. It is no secret what God can do."*

Thank you for taking this journey with us and remember with God you are never alone. In the next few pages you will read about a woman losing a spouse to cancer. A pastor losing four children to a congenital heart disease while another reveals hope after hurt depicting a faithful father raising a special needs child. Be *blown away* by a U.S. Marine who lost limbs fighting for our freedom and today walking with God and leading tens of thousands to faith in Christ now serving in the Lord's Army. Read about a Hollywood actress share about the pain of losing her father in death as a child only to be molested by a relative later. She walks on the red carpet publicly today as an adult but cried her eyes out privately as a child on her carpet first. We see her celebrity but God saw her in anonymity. You view the victory but Christ was near in calamity. Truly, God "bottles our tears" and near to the broken heart. Others have endured disease, some divorce and all disappointment but each author records that God was faithful through their storms. This account is a "*story behind the story-tellers.*"

The baby is now born and thanks to God's great grace the birth was right on-time. This is an "on-time" word for you and together let's rock the world for Jesus, The Rock. Your disappointment is a Divine Appointment and your setbacks are no longer viewed a demotion but a promotion from the Prince of Peace. You are not forgotten but destined to do great things and the parade didn't pass you by but God is coming down the street and He's asking YOU now to lead the way for His Second Coming.

Spectators are no longer needed but soldiers are being commissioned. God has guided you to this moment, your moment to help others not miss theirs but more importantly not miss THEIR appointment with Him. The Coach has called for you, God is the playbook and today you graduate from the bleachers into the game. "PLAY BALL!" Block out the critics and focus on Christ. **God doesn't make mistakes. He just corrects them and uses them for His glory.** Truly, I found a blessing in *being broken* and may you realize that your brokenness is a beautiful blessing from God.

"Count it all Joy!"
Frank Shelton, Jr.

Chapter One

"A star with scars"

BRENDA EPPERSON – Los Angeles, CA
www.BrendaEpperson.com

Brenda was born in North Hollywood California. Her late father, Kentucky born Don Epperson, was both a country singer (charted on RCA/VICTOR) with two top 10 hits, *Sittin on the Highway* with Glen Campbell singing background, Don Epperson also co starred with John Wayne in *Big Jake*. After his sudden death in 1973, (he was 32) Brenda's mother Sherry, was left alone to raise two daughters, Brenda and Deborah. A few years later the three of them left Southern California and moved to Dallas, Oregon, a small logging town of 6,000 people where Brenda spent most of her childhood. Shortly after that Brenda became a Christian at young age and found her forever father Jesus Christ. Sherry always told the girls that with God nothing is impossible. Brenda's favorite author at the time was Ann Keimel, her book, *I'm Out To Change My World,* and that's exactly what Brenda set out to do, one soul at a time. Brenda started speaking and singing at a young age to various youth groups and encouraging kids.

Early on Brenda had a passion for singing, she started singing in her church as well as various other churches and organizations and in High School was chosen as one of the youngest for a jazz vocal group winning numerous awards. Upon graduation high school Brenda toured the Far East singing for the King of Thailand as well as other dignitaries. Upon her return she decided to reach for the stars, with only $100 in her pocket and a big dream and a big God, Brenda went back to Los Angeles. Within a few years Brenda landed the lead on the **CBS** series *The Young and The Restless*, where she portrayed Ashley Abbott for more than seven years.

Brenda began her film career, starring in the **HBO** romantic comedy, *AMORE*, where she portrayed a singer, and performed a song on the soundtrack. Then, she co-starred with Swoozie Kurtz in the children's movie *STORYBOOK*. Brenda also starred with Ted McGinley and Leah Remini in the **LIFETIME** romantic comedy *FOLLOW YEAR HEART*, where Brenda performed two songs on the soundtrack along with Anita Pointer, (Pointer Sisters) and Phillip Ingram. Brenda was honored to win the coveted Angel Award for best song *If You Believe*.

Brenda has had the opportunity to appear on many magazine covers, such as **Woman World, TV Guide, Soap Opera Digest**, as well as many other magazines that included extensive stories on Brenda's life and career. **People Magazine** did a five page spread on her wedding, **Allo!, French Telepoche, USA Today, LA Times**, and many more. Brenda has also been featured on multiple entertainment and news programs across the country including **Oprah, CNN, CBS Morning news, TBN, The Howie Mandel Show, E! Entertainment, PAX, and Good Morning New York** to name a few.

Brenda also was chosen to sing two songs on the soundtrack for the limited release movie *KNOCKOUT*, along with Jose Feliciano and The Winans. Brenda then signed a recording contract with *SONY TRI/STAR LTC*, where, as a recording artist, she toured all over Europe as the opening act for **LIONEL RICHIE.** Brenda has enjoyed touring to different youth groups and women's groups across the country sharing her faith and encouraging others. To learn more, bookings, or reach out to me personally, go to www.BrendaEpperson.com or www.youtube.com/user/epprsn8 to view my music videos, www.itunes.com. Enter Brenda Epperson in the search box to download my songs and hopefully be encouraged or simply 'friend' me on Facebook! I've also, recently took the plunge and can now be reached on Twitter @BrendaEpperson

MY name is Brenda Epperson. I may be best known for the role I played as Ashley Abbott for over 7 years on the CBS daytime soap opera, "The Young and The Restless," as well as my musical journey signing with Sony TRISTAR/LTC and touring with Grammy Winner Lionel Richie as his opening act in Europe.

Recently, God has been doing a new thing in my life by sending me out speaking to women's ministries, churches and college groups sharing my story as well as the love of Christ. I've been broken more times than I care to say, but when I look back I'm so thankful. Here's where my story begins.

I had a very normal childhood with my mother, father and older sister, a house, a dog....until one day when my world was rocked. My father, the late Don Epperson RCA/Victor Recording artist, left the house one morning to catch his early "movie" call. He kissed his two sleeping girls on the head goodbye and never came home. I was 71/2 years old. Upon waking I heard what I thought was a seal that had landed right inside my living room. Little did I know it was the horrific cries of my very own grief stricken mother, receiving news that my father was in a fatal car accident in New Mexico. I jumped out of bed, ran down the hallway and found my mother sobbing with her head in her hands. As I said "Mommy?" she looked up at me, her face red and wet with tears and said, "Your father is dead!" I don't remember what happened next, only to wake up in the lap of the neighbor.

The next thing I knew my sister and I began walking down the street to a neighbors house to shelter us from the confusion. I'll never forget the anger that came over me as I waved my fist in the air and said, "I hate you God!" In that moment, at such a young age, I vowed to never cry again. That was it! That was the open door Satan needed to start hardening my heart toward God, myself and others.

You see, I was also carrying a very painful secret. Prior to my dad's sudden death, a boy had sexually molested me right inside our very own home. I was broken, numb, and filled with pain, sorrow and confusion. I never told anyone. My dad's death seemed to ignite the flames that caused an explosion of pain in my soul. I was left with very little self worth – I was so very broken. I kept my vow… when we'd visit Daddy's gravesite I didn't cry. The anger was kindled and began to grow. I grew up going to church but I didn't have a personal relationship with Christ. It all seemed very ceremonial to me. Jesus was just a guy in a picture that looked like he was nice to kids and animals, especially sheep! After my father's death our whole lives changed. Since he had just cancelled his life insurance policy because of finances, we were virtually left with nothing. In a very short time period everything I had was gone; my dad, our house, my school, friends, neighbors, local ice cream store and my dad's favorite white chair. I thank God for my Aunt Joey and, late Uncle Ronald B. Knoll, who moved us in with them to our new home in Winnemucca, Nevada - a far cry from Hollywood, California!

I hated my new school and made no friends, but always looked forward to coming home to play with my cousins, Mom, my sister Aunt and Uncle. I knew once I was home there would always be love and laughter even in the midst of our tears. As a youth, I was a heavy child - eating was a way of escape and comfort for me. I'll never forget my aunt, uncle and cousins talking so often about God and this 'personal relationship' thing. It was very foreign to me but seemed so real to them.

Then Christmas eve, at a candle light service in a tiny Assembly of God Church on a dusty road in the middle of nowhere, I stood next to my Uncle Ron who had become a great father figure in my life. We all stood in prayer with candles in our hands and I felt this overwhelming sense of love and peace come over me like nothing I'd ever felt before. That night at the age of 9, as tears streamed down my face, I accepted Jesus Christ into my heart. The sadness and anger didn't all leave right away, but I started to realize that I wasn't alone anymore. Suddenly I knew God was always with me, He had always loved me, even though I didn't love myself.

My uncle was eventually transferred to an even smaller town called Dallas, Oregon, population 6,000, so we moved with them. My new school and 5th grade class was filled with even more challenges. I was still angry and bigger than ever reaching a hefty size 16 and still hated myself. I would have thoughts that it was my fault my daddy died, and I was being punished because of what that boy had done to me. Kids incessantly teased me about my weight – a boy on his bike even spit on my friend and I while walking home. He yelled some horrible name as he and his friend raced by. As my anger increased, my self esteem decreased. I was constantly in fights at school, mostly with boys, with frequent visits to the principal's office! During this time through my mothers' wisdom and faithful prayers we found our new church. Slowly, the word of God was poured into my life and my healing began. When thoughts of unworthiness came I began to recognize they were lies from the enemy and I would answer back, "That's not what God says about me! That's not who God says I am!

You see, as I heard the word of God, the light of Christ began to fill up those very dark places inside my soul and in my life. I began to really know that God loves me! God's love began to penetrate, heal and light up those dark, even secret places in my life and the healing began. Miraculously, I even cried in church from time to time. God softened the very depths of my soul and replaced my grieving with healing tears and so much joy! I remember looking in the mirror at one point and actually liking myself for a quick moment. As Gods love and light moved within me, the dark places began to leave. I began to like myself little by little, and soon I lost weight. I auditioned for events while trying out for sports and leadership positions in high school.

When I truly believed my worth was in Christ and Christ alone, I became be more accepted at school while making healthy friendships – some of which have continued through the years. Eventually, I did tell my Mom what had happened which was healing for all of us.

I thank God because in my personal *brokenness*, I have experienced healing, restoration, newness, hope and God's amazing grace. This is often costly, painful and difficult. I remember times I could barely get out of bed to face another day! We can be broken in many ways, physically, through divorce, death of a loved one, or addiction, but I have realized that through everything we all have a choice!

We can remain unbroken in our comfort zone and in pain if we'd like, but when we choose to say 'YES' to Christ he begins to break us and mold us so we can be healed and put back together in his image, not ours. If we remain unbroken we have no impact or affect for God, or for others around us in this world.

I have learned in my life tears are not a sign of weakness, they are beautiful! Tears are a sign of compassion, tenderness and love. Here is a beautiful quote from a highly influential writer and theologian, Frederick Buechner from his book Whistling In the Dark. "Whenever you find tears in your eyes, especially unexpected tears, it's well to pay closets attention. They are not only telling a secret of who you are, but more often then not of the mystery of where you have come from and are summoning you to where you should go next."

Those negative painful thoughts eventually left completely, and the tears and hard heartedness began to disappear. I love this verse in Psalms 34:18 **"God's grace is most present in the lives of the weak and broken. The Lord is close to the broken hearted and saves those who are crushed in spirit."** (NIV)

I don't know about you, but when something's broken or if I break something and can't fix it, I usually throw it away, put it to the side, or just forget about it....give up on it. I thank God in heaven He didn't do that with me! He was closest to me in my brokenness. He never gave up on me nor did he put me to the side even though I gave up on Him and myself. He will never, ever give up on you either. God loves you so very much!

Deuteronomy 31:8
"The Lord himself goes before you and will be with you; he will never leave you nor forsake you. Do not be afraid; do not be discouraged" (NIV)

Chapter Two

"The Gift of Failure"

SAM GLENN – NAPERVILLE, IL
www.SamGlenn.com

Sam Glenn hails from Naperville, IL just outside of Chicago, IL and has inspired over three million people in person with his amazing story. He has spoken to audiences as large as 75,000 and was speaker for two years with Ron Luce & Teen Mania's "Acquire the Fire." He spoke at the largest Youth Event in America "DAY ONE" and has done event with the Billy Graham Evangelistic Association and countless organizations.

Sam is the leading authority on Attitude and coaches corporations on how to excel in encouragement. Sam shares HUMOR, life lessons and closes out each session with a chalk drawing masterpiece that mesmerizes audiences across America. His radio program LEADERSHIP UNIVERSITY is ideal for all who desire to graduate from mediocrity. He is the author of 15 books and been featured in Fox News Business, Chicago Tribune, Assoc Press & hundreds more! Sam is a CEO and authority on "Everything Attitude!" and spoken to

Fortune 500 companies across America and led several chapels for both NFL and NBA.

WHEN people often ask me how I got to where I am, my response is that I am a good failure. I normally get an odd look at first, but then I explain what a good failure is. *A good failure is someone who doesn't waste his trials, but absorbs the valuable lessons that come from them and uses them as stepping stones.* When you examine the profile of those who have achieved a great level of success doing what they are passionate about, you learn that the success didn't usually come without a price tag. There was failure involved, and there were humbling lessons to be learned. I have observed that in order to get to where you want to be and achieve what you really want, it's okay to fail; but when you do, your response to that failure becomes crucial to what happens next.

I could see the stairs out my car window. It was clear, and not too hot for a July evening. When you are alone with your thoughts, many things can happen. You can begin to look at your situation and past mistakes and really beat yourself up, or you can examine what is amazing about you and determine to dream big dreams. Going after my dreams seemed next to impossible as I gazed up at the stars from the backseat of my '82 Buick Regal. I didn't have anywhere else to go as I didn't have a place of my own. I was broke, and yes, some nights I slept in the back of my car. If it wasn't in my car, it was on the floor in my mom's apartment.

So you ask, how did things get so bad? We don't always make perfect choices, but the key is to learn from the ones that are not the best for you. I would say that I had made choices that made things bad. Initially, I did what I was told to do. I went to college, got a degree and applied for jobs. It was hard for me, however, to accept a position working for someone else given that I had such a strong entrepreneurial spirit. I felt called to run my own business, although it didn't seem like that would become the case.

When my grandfather, Richard Albertson, passed away in 1989, however, he left our family his business to run. It was a small company that he oversaw for close to thirty years. He came up with an idea for wild birds called Nest-Aid, selling nesting material for wild birds (like those that you find flying around your backyard). Little did I know that the wild bird market—bird houses, bird seed, etc.—was a multi-billion-dollar-per-year business. I also discovered that the number-one hobby in America was gardening, and number two was birding. It was a unique market. We took over Gramps' business to the best that we could. It was seasonal, so my grandpa was able to buy himself a huge RV to travel all over the United States and visit his kids and grandkids.

I saw a lot of potential in the business, so I basically took up the mantel and started working on expanding it. I had no idea what I was doing, but I was able to grow the business and go to school at the same time. School is a great place to get book smart, but I had the good fortune of getting street smart at the same time. This gave me a huge leg up in the so called "real world." However, when you don't really know what you are doing, that leg up can find a way to be a leg in your backside.

I struggled to figure things out. I borrowed so much money and applied it to ideas that didn't pay off. So I found myself in a heap of dept and not sure what to do. The answer came one July afternoon when a woman called and informed me that the warehouse that housed all my product and assembly had burned to the ground. Just like that, everything was lost. There was no insurance—nothing.

I was about to face the biggest lesson of my life—how to deal with failure. I have to admit that I didn't deal with it very well at first. I was so depressed, which is a natural human response when something doesn't work out. However, I sat in my depression for quite a while. I began to fear trying again. I would blame others for my situation. I wasn't responsible enough to own what had happened. I went from being happy and excited about what life had to offer, to being broken and sad. All I wanted to do was sleep and not wake up. I was embarrassed that I had destroyed my grandfather's work of more than thirty years. There was no way to recover. It was over and done. Things seemed to change for me when my brother invited me to volunteer at a youth group in Oak Brook, Illinois. I really didn't know what to do, but I hung out with teens in a place where there would be a message delivered, and then time to just mingle. It may not have seemed like anything really big, but I learned a very powerful Scripture verse from the Bible: **"Many are the plans in a man's heart, but it is the Lord's purpose that prevails."** -Proverbs 19:21

God seemed to have a different plan for me than the one I had lived up until then. After volunteering for a short time, I was asked if I would teach Sunday school. I wanted to, but was scared. I was afraid of public speaking, and concerned that what I had to say really didn't matter. Again, God had a different opinion and agenda. The first Sunday I got to teach, I was so scared that I even thought about canceling.

The class started at eight a.m., and I was up at four a.m. debating if I should cancel. There was a tug of war in my heart and mind. But I did it and it was awesome! My speaking wasn't that polished, but encouraging others and lifting them up was amazing! I found a renewed purpose and passion for my life: I would encourage others.

It would be a few more years from that initial realization when my dream of speaking in front of audiences and inspiring them to not give up and to follow their calling would happen in a bigger way (I have since spoken for crowds as large as 75,000, and make my living inspiring corporate groups nationwide). However, the process itself is was what became my classroom. I learned so much about myself and life through my hardships. God opened my eyes to realize that I may fail, but that is okay. We should not waste our failures. We should learn from them and use them as stepping stones. I did just that.

Today, I have authored several books and encouraged millions of people through speeches. So when you ask me how I got here...all I can say is I am a *good failure*.

Chapter Three

"Beyond Brokenness"

JAMEY RAGLE – CINCINNATI, OH
www.JameyRagle.com

For over three decades Jamey Ragle has inspired audiences in small country churches and some of the largest arenas across America. Jamey began singing with the Dixie Melody Boys in the 1970's, and soon began speaking and conducting Crusades, Conferences, and The Jamey Ragle Comedy Café. Jamey has been featured on TBN, PTL & Living the Life. His passion for breaking down the age barrier and denominational walls has enabled him to share the stage with Chris Tomlin, Todd Agnew, Jeff Foxworthy, actor Steven Baldwin and many more.

He has spoken for the United States Navy in Japan, at the Western States Quartet Convention in California, and in hundreds of churches. Jamey has recorded numerous music projects and signature messages such as "Have a Blast While You Last", "Slaying the Dragon of Your Past", and "Dear Dr. Phil". Jamey continues to travel America passionately sharing the message of love, healing, and hope. Jamey's hilarious comedic style of communication will uplift and inspire. Someone described Jamey as a mix between Larry the Cable Guy, Dr. Phil and Billy Graham. Dr. Falwell once said that hearing Jamey is like having open heart surgery, while being fully conscious, and enjoying every minute of it! Jamey is currently holding "Preach the Word" meetings with Gold City Quartet, as well as one day meetings, three day crusades, and The Comedy Café. Jamey shares from his heart how we can take the journey from brokenness to wholeness and breathe. God is using Jamey greater than ever and for more info www.JameyRagle.com

\\\

BEYOND *BROKENNESS*. After more than three decades of ministry, I took leave of my senses. I hopped aboard the crazy train and stepped into stupid; I became someone I never imagined myself to be. I am not so sure the dynamics of how I got there are important, but it is sad to say that human beings are mesmerized by details .The truth of the matter is, your friends do not care and your enemies only want details to fuel their fodder.

What I have learned in this journey beyond brokenness is twofold. The first thing is that mere brokenness is not enough for some people to be ultimately compliant to the Holy Spirit. In other words, with sheer human ingenuity, some effort and superglue (if you will), some situations can be fixed. My life, however, needed more than superglue. I did not need a human fix. I had to journey beyond brokenness. That's right! God took me on a journey. Now, make no mistake about it; it was my own foolish decisions and my own foolish choices that precipitated this journey. But, it was a journey that would take me beyond brokenness. It was a journey of utter despair.

Despair, by the way, opens a doorway to an intimate place with God that no other human emotion can open. This desperation is the kind of desperation that Jairus experienced at the death of his daughter. It is the kind of desperation that Mary and Martha communicated with Jesus when they cried, "Jesus, your friend and our brother is near death, and if you do not get here he's going to die. Jesus, you *must* get here!"

The woman in the gospel that was hemorrhaging to death bullied her way through the crowds to get to Jesus out of desperation (Mark 5:25-34). Now, there were many noble and "worthy" distractions to get in her way but her frame of mind was, "Look, I love you all. I appreciate you and I thank you for the invitation to the baby shower, but if you do not get out of the way I am going to run you over because I *have* to get to Jesus!" My friend, desperation is the posture that is going to take you beyond brokenness.

If you are to ever move beyond brokenness to usefulness, there are some things you *must* know.

I. There is a difference in living and operating out of sheer talent and effort and living and operating under the powerful anointing of the Holy Spirit.

Our survival depends on it. If you and I are ever to see a life of usefulness and purpose beyond brokenness, we must be willing to live and walk under the anointing of God through the Holy Spirit. So many people live their entire lives not yielded because they have never been beyond brokenness. For instance, there is a difference between talent and anointing. Oftentimes, those in ministry want to believe that we live and operate in the realm of the anointing. The truth is, often, our effort is human and it is nothing more than sheer talent. Sadly, many have talent that can take them where their character cannot keep them.

II. If we are to move beyond brokenness, we must quit playing the victim and view ourselves as victors.

Here is the deal. Most people have excuses for why they made the choices they made. Are you kidding me? I watched and listened the other day as a 500-pound person said to me, "Jamey, I am 500 pounds, but it's not what I am eating...it's what's eating me." No, Brother, it *is* what you are eating! None of us can eat an entire pie before bed and expect not to struggle with a few extra pounds! There is no logical way to place the blame on any external factor that can take credit for a 500-pound, life-threatening physical condition! This person's only desire was to point fingers and accept failure! The truth is, blaming whatever it is that is eating him will only get him further and further into a life of obesity and unhappiness!

Something else to consider is this: the day you boarded the crazy train and stepped into stupid, you signed up for the good, the bad and the ugly. I had a friend who had taken much the same journey as mine tell me not long ago that people were lying about him. He said that he did not really do what he had been accused of doing. Just like my friend, you must quit playing the victim. You signed up for that! The day you chose a path independent of God, you signed up for the true and the false. Unfortunately, human beings are mesmerized by details and are not particularly concerned of whether or not those details are accurate. Moving beyond brokenness must involve the realization that your destructive decisions will not go away. But, those same decisions are going to be the walkway that guides you to a stronger, truer relationship with God!

III. Most of us have friends for a reason, friends for a season, and very few friends for a lifetime.

There were many discoveries I made on my own journey beyond brokenness. I was deafened by the silence of my "friends." We, as full-time ministers, were all so quick to preach grace and restoration but slow to model it. Now, please do not get me wrong. I am not seeking sympathy or throwing my own pity party. In my journey beyond brokenness, I have owned my actions and I have accepted that I will never portray myself as a victim. The facts are the facts, though. Sadly enough, you do not have as many true friends as you thought you had.

When you are at your darkest, your loneliest, and your most ashamed time, you will have no other choice but to run desperately to Jesus. The hemorrhaging woman ignored the crowed and pushed through to Jesus. Mary and Martha sought comfort and help from no other source but Jesus. Even The Savior himself left his disciples to speak with God, because only God's grace and wisdom were sufficient in Jesus' darkest, most worrisome moments. There will be people in your life that desire to show empathy and understanding of your shame, but you must desperately seek out the one who gave his own life for yours before you can truly find peace beyond brokenness.

IV. If we are to ever move beyond our brokenness, there must be genuine conviction and contrition.

This, my friend, may be the hardest pill to swallow for some. You see, there must be change in direction that's precipitated by conviction and contrition but not consequence. Many people are sorry because they are caught, not because they are convicted. The Bible says in Psalms that, **"The Lord is near to those who have a broken heart, and saves such as have a contrite spirit."** Contrition involves sincere and absolute remorse. It is a hatred of your iniquities and refers to a brokenness that must be repaired. To move beyond brokenness, a person *must* have such a spirit of contrition that only God can restore.

In Isaiah, the Bible says, "My hands have made both heaven and earth; they and everything in them are mine. I, the LORD, have spoken! I will bless those who have humble and contrite hearts, who tremble at my word." What does man gain eternally if the creator of the world and everything in it blesses those who are humble, self-denying, and detest sin so greatly that they maintain a spirit of contrition? To move beyond brokenness, you must deny yourself and repent of your iniquities. You must seek the renewal of the Holy Spirit. You must know that, like the Psalmist writes, the Lord saves those with a contrite spirit and you can continue beyond brokenness with hope and optimism.

V. If we are to move beyond brokenness, we must not let our failures define our lives!

To move beyond brokenness, the most important thing to remember is that no matter what you have done or no matter how deep the stain of your sin, there is no pit so deep where God's love is not deeper still. Those words by Corrie ten Boom resonate so softly in my heart as I continue on my journey beyond brokenness. Listen friend, you still have a future with God!

If you are to move beyond brokenness, you must not let your failure define your life. You must let God's forgiveness facilitate your future. Here is the deal: those who are complacent in their failure view a weak moment as a monument. It defines their life. "Oh, *that's* the guy that was convicted of manslaughter." "*That's* the guy that committed adultery." "*That's* the woman that had an abortion." My friend, failure is but a moment. What we consider a catastrophe, God considers a classroom. God can teach us in only a moment of failure an entire lifetime of lesson.

So, here is the truth. Failing is but a moment. I cannot reiterate that enough! Do not let it be a monument that defines who you are. View your failure as a moment of foolishness and a moment that's costly but can also incur great gain. The Bible says in Proverbs, "The way of the transgressor is hard." So yes, it is very hard. But here is what we need to know. Jesus spoke these powerful words to Peter at The Last Supper as he prophesized Peter's betrayal: "But I have pleaded in prayer for you, Simon, that your faith should not fail. So when you have repented and turned to me again, strengthen your brothers (Luke 22:32)." Jesus knew how Peter would fail and betray the Son of God but encouraged him nonetheless. What an example of Jesus' mercy on his own offender!

David was called a man after God's own heart. God fully knew what David's actions would be, but God still called him a man after *his* heart. "The sacrifices of God are a broken spirit, a broken and a contrite heart, these O God, You will not despise." (Ps. 51:17) David prayed these words as a part of his repentance. He was remorseful and prayed with conviction. Because of his contrition, God forgave David and moved him beyond brokenness to a freedom that allowed him to compose the fifty-first Psalm eloquently his transgression and his repentance.

You have a future with God! To move beyond your brokenness, I encourage you to let your greatest source of council and considerations come from the Word of God! The Scripture tells us that our sins and our iniquities have been buried in the sea of forgetfulness. They have been forgiven! They have been blotted out! I move on and I live and walk in freedom today, not because I deserve it, but because the one that gave his own life for me provided a way out.

My prayer for you, my friend, is that you will move beyond brokenness to a place of freedom. I pray that you will allow God's forgiveness to embellish your life with hope and anticipation. I pray that, in the midst of friends that become strangers and acquaintances that amplify your darkest regrets, you will find a friend that loves you regardless of your failure. I am eternally grateful to my pastor friend Gene Wolfenbarger and the membership of The Gathering in Pigeon Forge, TN for throwing me a lifeline. They embraced me and were mightily used in my restoration. But above all, my only hope can come from the God of this universe who knew my sin before I did yet still granted me an opportunity to move beyond brokenness. My friend, He will do the very same for you.

Chapter Four

"Dying in Georgia to Atlanta Live"

SHELLEY HENDRIX – ATLANTA, GA
www.Church4Chicks.com

Shelley Hendrix is a wife, mother, teacher, speaker, author, and television talk show host. But more important than any role she fills, she is most grateful to know beyond a shadow of a doubt that she belongs to and matters to God. Recognizing her value, worth, significance, and security come directly as a gift of God's grace, and not of her own striving or self-effort, has dramatically changed her life. She desires to be a voice of truth to this generation, pouring her life into others that she might be used of God to create hunger for God and His Word in as many lives as possible. She is a host of "Atlanta Live!" - A Christian Talk Show on Atlanta's WATC TV 57, and has been a featured guest on radio programs around the nation and Fox News Live. Shelley speaks at various events nationally and internationally, and was also a contributing writer to "Secrets of Confidence"- a devotional book for women published by Barbour Publishing. Shelley's first published book is entitled "On Purpose For A Purpose," which can be used for individual or group study and is based from the Book of Esther. Also available is her 31-day devotional guide called "Wisdom: A Girl's Best Friend," based on the Proverbs. Her current project in the works is "Why Can't We All Just Get Along?!" which will be published by Harvest House Publishers. Additionally, Shelley is also a freelance writer and has been published with Randall House Publishing and various other publications and blogs.

Shelley received her certificate of counseling at First Baptist Woodstock, GA in 2005, trained under the leadership of the Director of Counseling, Rev. James Eubanks. She has also received certificates from CLASS Speakers Training he has also received certificates from CLASS Speakers Training Seminar as well as the SCORRE Conference (FKA "Dynamic Communicator's Workshop"), led by Ken Davis and Michael Hyatt. Shelley will readily tell you that one of the greatest honors of her life is being married to her best friend, Stephen Hendrix, CADC, Director of Clinical Programs for the HopeQuest Ministries Group, Inc.; A counseling ministry to men and women struggling with life dominating issues such as drug addiction, alcohol addiction, and sexual brokenness. They have two teenage daughters and one spunky 9 year old son (whom God uses to teach them much!) and travel from Atlanta, Georgia. Learn more at www.Church4Chicks.com

---

I'LL never forget sitting on the edge of my bed, feeling completely hopeless. Completely defeated. Completely broken. I'll never forget crying out to God, "All I ever wanted was to be someone You could use in my generation....what can You possibly do with me now?"

Although it has been 12 years since that time in my life, it is a memory as fresh to me as any I made this week. From the time I was very young, I have known about God and loved Him with as much of my heart as I could. As I think back on my earliest memories, I see a thread weaved throughout my childhood, teen years, and young adulthood. I always wanted to be pleasing to those I loved and admired. Looking back now, I realize I equated success in pleasing people to pleasing God. Trouble was I never felt like anyone in my life was ever truly pleased with me.

As a child, my family went to church very regularly—and that's actually putting it pretty mildly! Truth be told, my dad was a pastor of our home church and we lived smack dab on the church's property! In fact, for one year, when we lived in Tampa, FL, our family of five resided in a one room/one bathroom furlough bedroom inside of the church we attended! Our lives were literally consumed by "church." My understanding of being a Christian had to do with rules that needed to be kept, and those rules kept getting stricter and stricter as time went by.

I'll never forget the time I wanted to know what it felt like to say a cuss word. I was such a people pleaser, but I wanted to rebel, I guess, so I snuck myself into the church bus (on the property shared with our mobile home) and I whispered, "Gosh," "Golly," and "Gee." I kid you not. And, I actually felt a little surprised that I wasn't struck down by lightning soon afterward. My whole life was consumed with Church and with trying to figure out all the myriad of ways to strive to please a Holy, Just, and Righteous—not to mention Omnipotent—God. That is, until I was about 10 years old.

It's a long story that would take up far too much time to tell, so suffice it to say, after years of ministering to others, and dealing with private pain and shame themselves (with no safe people to turn to in their own times of suffering), my parents resigned completely from ministry, and it wasn't too much longer before they resigned from church, too. It was a bizarre and confusing time. In order to get just a taste of how bizarre and confusing this period of my life was, you'd also have to know that not only had we been a ministry family—we were a *different sort* of ministry family. For example, we were not allowed to own a TV or go to movies.

None of us wore shorts, and the girls in the family didn't wear pants either. (Culottes were allowed then, and I can tell you now: I don't think I could force myself to wear another pair of culottes if my life depended on it!) During the years of E.T. and Star Wars, my brothers and I had to be content getting the run-down from our friends whose parents didn't believe it was a sin to go to the movies. My understanding of God was basically that He was watching our every move like a strict probation officer—expecting me to screw up and determined to catch and punish me when I did.

How in the world does anyone please a being like that? Although I had such little success at it, I was determined that one day, somehow, I would muster up enough of whatever it was that was missing, and I would finally make my Heavenly Father proud that I was His own.

Although we sang about God's love and we memorized John 3:16, I somehow missed the message that I had a Heavenly Father who deeply delighted in me—simply because it's in His nature do so. It never crossed my mind that He actually loved me—just as I was.

When my parents stopped taking us to church, they didn't make any kind of announcement about it. They just stopped getting us up for church. At first, I loved this! It felt like freedom to sleep in, watch cartoons (now that we were allowed to have a TV), and be like other kids I went to school with. I remember asking my mom at one point if we were going to go back to church. I remember her response as though she just said it, "We've decided to see how the other half lives for a while." Looking back, I realize we saw far more than any of us ever bargained for.

Several years went by and we didn't go to church. Other family members were concerned, and our parents coached us kids in how to respond to those concerns when they were voiced to us outside of their presence. I often felt like I was the rope in the middle of a tug of war fight. On the one side, I felt the tugging of well meaning people as well as my own conscience and what I believed to be "right," and on the other, the tug of my culture to conform and find acceptance. I lived in the middle of this tension for several years.

Finally, in the middle of my 9th grade year, my best friend invited me to a youth retreat at a church she didn't even attend—but the boy she was crushing on *did* go to that church. So, of course she needed someone there for moral support, and who better than a bestie? Right? I can see now how God had His hand in that whole thing. From the time I arrived, the people of that church—a different denomination than what I had been a part of—warmly embraced me and accepted me as one of their own. I loved that whole weekend and began attending that church. (Of course the fact that I had a huge crush on the youth pastor didn't hurt, either! God will use whatever He's got to use!)

In a very short amount of time, I went from taking steps down a dark path, to finding myself walking on firmer ground—and not by myself. Although my time spent at that church also included several heartbreaking and challenging circumstances, I will always be grateful for that small church on Highway 92 in Woodstock, Georgia for being there when I needed them to be.

I began to grow spiritually, and for a while felt God's pleasure because, for the most part, the people there accepted me and made me feel more at home than I had ever felt since I was a little girl. I began to have personal convictions about integrity, purity, and a real commitment to Jesus Christ. In the years that followed, I became a leader in my youth group and in my school. It's amazing what a little acceptance from folks can do for a very insecure and shy person! I wanted to know what I believed and why I believed it. What I had been taught for most of my life didn't seem to work for my parents, so I began to consume the Word of God like never before. I would spend hours studying my dad's old concordances and study guides. It wasn't like today when you could just hop online to get information. You actually had to search it out for yourself!

It was during those teen years that I fell in love with the Bible. It was in those years that my parents divorced. It was in those years that I got my heart broken a few times. It was during those teen years that I fell in love with someone. It was even in those teen years that I got engaged and got married. I said "no" to college scholarships and an offer to study abroad and I said "I do" on October 10, 1992. I don't believe in putting other people's "stuff" out there without their consent and blessing, so I won't go into what all went wrong in my marriage. I can tell you, though, that two things went right! Their names are Amelia and Macey. I will always be grateful to God for putting a man in my life who would make it possible for me to be the mother of those two wonderful girls.

In those short 6 ½ years of marriage, life was like a roller coaster ride for me. If I felt I had my husband's love, acceptance and affirmation, I was enjoying the ride! But when I didn't, and this was more often than not, I dealt with great despair and loneliness. Not knowing what to do put me into a cycle of trying harder and doing better, but never feeling like I had gained any real momentum or that I was on the path to success. I held onto the belief that if I would be faithful to my vows and to my God, then one day, it would be worth it all. I really never expected it to end. Hindsight truly is 20/20 and now I realize why my divorce wasn't as big of a surprise to everyone else that it was to me.

For a world-class, card-carrying people pleaser, this was the worst thing I could ever imagine happening to me. It seems that there is a prevailing thought in the Church today that there are really only 2 great sins any believer can commit: abortion and divorce. For whatever reason, these two "sins" seem to carry far more weight and lasting shame for believers than just about anything else. In January, 1999, my husband told me he didn't love me, that he had never really loved me, and that he wanted out. I wish I could tell you that I had been the perfect wife to him and that he had no reason to be unhappy with me, but I can't.

I wasn't perfect then and I'm certainly not perfect now. I didn't want to accept his wishes and I fought with everything in me to regain his favor and invite him back into our marriage. In March of 1999, it became evident this was not going to happen. And, so this brings us back to me sitting on the edge of my bed, crying out to God, "How in the world can You use me now?" I couldn't imagine there was anything of value I could ever offer in the walls of a church because—based on someone else's actions—I was now 'damaged goods.' It definitely didn't help that there were people coming to me at church, in the grocery store, and over the phone trying to counsel me in all different directions.

Some of the best advice I got came from a woman named Lisa. I'll never forget her saying, "Shelley, stay in the Word. Don't get a book on divorce…stay in the Word of God!" As I sat there on my bed, I had my Bible laid open before me. I don't remember how I came to this passage, I only know that God meant for me to read it. It's a bit long, but I want you to read it, too, so I'm including it here.

¹ In you, LORD, I have taken refuge;
let me never be put to shame.
² In your righteousness, rescue me and deliver me;
turn your ear to me and save me.
³ Be my rock of refuge,
to which I can always go;
give the command to save me,
for you are my rock and my fortress.

⁴ Deliver me, my God, from the hand of the wicked,
from the grasp of those who are evil and cruel.
⁵ For you have been my hope, Sovereign LORD,
my confidence since my youth.
⁶ From birth I have relied on you;
you brought me forth from my mother's womb.
I will ever praise you.
⁷ I have become a sign to many;
you are my strong refuge.
⁸ My mouth is filled with your praise,
declaring your splendor all day long.
⁹ Do not cast me away when I am old;
do not forsake me when my strength is gone.
¹⁰ For my enemies speak against me;
those who wait to kill me conspire together.
¹¹ They say, "God has forsaken him;
pursue him and seize him,
for no one will rescue him."
¹² Do not be far from me, my God;
come quickly, God, to help me.
¹³ May my accusers perish in shame;
may those who want to harm me
be covered with scorn and disgrace.
¹⁴ As for me, I will always have hope;
I will praise you more and more.
¹⁵ My mouth will tell of your righteous deeds,
of your saving acts all day long—
though I know not how to relate them all.
¹⁶ I will come and proclaim your mighty acts,
Sovereign LORD;
I will proclaim your righteous deeds, yours alone.
¹⁷ Since my youth, God, you have taught me,
and to this day I declare your marvelous deeds.
¹⁸ Even when I am old and gray,
do not forsake me, my God,

till I declare your power to the next generation,
your mighty acts to all who are to come.
¹⁹ *Your righteousness, God, reaches to the heavens,*
you who have done great things.
Who is like you, God?
²⁰ *Though you have made me see troubles,*
many and bitter,
you will restore my life again;
from the depths of the earth
you will again bring me up.
²¹ *You will increase my honor*
and comfort me once more.
²² *I will praise you with the harp*
for your faithfulness, my God;
I will sing praise to you with the lyre,
Holy One of Israel.
²³ *My lips will shout for joy*
when I sing praise to you—
I whom you have delivered.
²⁴ *My tongue will tell of your righteous acts*
all day long,
for those who wanted to harm me
have been put to shame and confusion.
Psalm 71 New International Version, ©2010 (NIV)

As I read and re-read this passage, I knew God had me in mind when He had the Psalmist write it. I don't believe for a second that I was the *only* one He had in mind, but I'm confident I was in there! As I read over the verses about not forsaking me until I can declare His works to the next generation, I wrote my daughter's names in the margin. I figured that although there were some in the Church that did not want me anymore, there was only one woman God made the mother of those precious girls, and I was going to do my job and do it to the best of my ability!

Verses 20-21, though, meant the most to me of all the verses contained here. I had been weeping before my Heavenly Father that I was afraid of the shame I was going to carry forevermore after because my husband no longer wanted me. I knew I wouldn't suffer shame much out in "the world," but I had already gotten a bitter taste in my mouth from well-meaning, but misinformed, folks in the Church. And, here God spoke so clearly, that if I would continue to praise Him anyways, and make His name great in my life, that not only would I *not* suffer shame, He was going to *increase* my honor! *That's grace!*

At that time I knew from the depths of my soul that this was from God. There was little doubt that God wanted to give me hope and the promise of a bright and fulfilling future—not one shrouded by a cloak of shame. Now that I'm over a decade down the road from that time, I can tell you that He has certainly exceeded any expectations this chick had at the time!

I wish I could tell you that I never let my God down after that point. I wish I could tell you the road became easier and the load became lighter. It didn't. There were still folks who felt I shouldn't be teaching youth at church anymore. "Kids don't need to be exposed to this sort of thing." When Stephen and I began dating there were plenty of folks telling me I had no business dating him (because they believed that since I had been married before it would make us both adulterers if we married.)

Stephen said to me once, "This makes no sense to me. I was out using drugs and people less than two years ago and I can walk the halls of a church with my head held high because of what Christ has done for me. But for you, people judge you because of what your husband chose to do—even though you were faithful to him. This makes no sense." Don't get me wrong, now. There were more people who were kind and supportive than those who were not, but those who were not were a bit louder and more persistent. I can tell you this: God continued to guide me. He continued to provide for my girls and me. He continued to protect us from too many things to include here. I was tempted to walk away from the Church during that season—but I'm so thankful I didn't.

God spoke to my heart in a clear way through that passage and others, and told me, "If you'll hang in there and remain faithful, I'm going to use this in the lives of the very ones who are hurting you." And, can I tell you that almost every single person who came against me during that time has since come back to apologize? Only God could do that. In

1999, I thought my life was over. I figured I'd be the Invisible Woman (at church anyways) for the rest of my life; hiding in the shadows so that I didn't upset others who's lives made God look so much better than mine did. But, my Father wouldn't hear of such a thing! Nope. Instead, he rebuilt my home with a new, more solid foundation when he brought Stephen Hendrix into our family. He gave me a son—one in whom my heart delights! And for several years, I was perfectly happy and content with these incredible, above my expectations and dreams, gifts.

But, then—as if that weren't enough—God went and surprised me even more! In 2004, He made it very clear to both Stephen and me that He had a call and purpose for me; one that was a huge shock! The only way I can describe the calling was that it's to be a voice of truth in my generation. The very thing I had wanted so long ago, God affirmed and then confirmed over and over and over as 2004 progressed.

In 2005, doors began to open for me to use my voice to speak truth into the lives of others. Each time I stood before a group—of any size—I would become so sick before hand. I was scared slap crazy! It was awful...until I stood up with microphone on and began to open my mouth. In that moment, something would click. Something would happen that I'd never experienced outside of my role as wife to Stephen and mother to my children: I knew that I knew that I knew I was born for this purpose!

Since 2005, God has continued to open new doors of opportunity. The journey has been the hardest of my life—and I'm not including that for dramatic effect either! The call has cost us so very much. But when I see the redemptive work of God's grace in the life of another who has been impacted by my story and the studies I teach whether at Church 4 Chicks or elsewhere; or the times I've hosted Atlanta Live here in my beautiful city—I know.

I know that I was born for this, and that all the things I went through in my struggle has been because God loves me, not in spite of the fact that He loves me. And, so He has taken me from a place of rejection to a place of honor, and only by His grace. By no means have I arrived. But, by no means am I where He found me either! In the Book of the Revelation, we're told that there will be people who will overcome insurmountable obstacles and opposition that position them for the great opportunities

God holds ready for those who are faithful. These people overcome with two things: The blood of the Lamb and the word of their testimony. (See Revelation 12:11) And when I take a look in the rearview mirror of my life and see where victory has been experienced, I also see these two realities: The precious blood of Jesus that paid it all and the testimony of my own changed life. Today I trust that the best is yet to come.

Chapter Five

"Born to Drum"

ANDY WILLIAMS ("Bald Wunda")
– McDonough, GA
www.SoulSisterSally.com &
www.CastingCrowns.com

Andy Williams (also "Bald Wunda") is a man with a message and on a mission.

He embodies fun and lives by faith. Andy was the drummer for Grammy Award Winner

Casting Crowns and after five years God led him to step out in faith and start "Soul Sister Sally."

His bride, Kelly is the lead vocalist and together they share interests in jazz, coffee, big cities, disc golf and Star Wars! Andy's favorite movie is The Sound of Music and loves to decorate, play football and longs to purchase a Harley Davidson in near future.

Soul Sister Sally is a eclectic group that reaches the masses with the message and hope of Jesus. They play at big and small venues and have a desire to help hurting people with their music. They reside in the Peach State with their AWESOME son, Aden.

Visit www.SoulSisterSally.com E-mail: andy@soulsistersally.com Facebook.com/baldwunda Twitter.com/baldwunda

ONCE upon a time, in a galaxy called Stockbridge, GA, there was a fairly young man playing drums at a youth church service. This was no ordinary youth service. This was one of those services where the worship was groovin and The Spirit was movin! I remember the young man playing the drums different than before, like he had a new passion for what he already loved to do. As the music was slowing down, a silent worship began to fill the room and the Holy Spirit took over. The drummer simply put his head down on his snare drum and started to weep in the presence of an amazing God.

He had never felt so peaceful and so loved and that's when the Lord spoke to me. The desire to play drums hit me when I was about 16 years old. A few of my friends played drums. I just thought the drums were the cat's pajamas and I absolutely had to try it! I sat down at different drum kits several different times and to my eternal dissatisfaction, I never could make it happen! I used to sit and listen to my mom and dad's 8 tracks. I would listen to their old records for hours on end. I could not wait for music class every week in elementary school! I just loved music!

I sang in the Atlanta Boy Choir for 3 years and I took piano lessons for almost 3 years and you would think musical experience like that would help, but not for this guy! When I was ready to graduate from high school, my mom asked me what I wanted for a graduation gift. I expectantly said "DRUMS!" and reluctantly threw in "or a keyboard", so she would have a choice. So, I got the keyboard and practiced on a regular basis with a repressed desire to jump on a drum kit and go berserk! I ended up playing keyboard and singing for my youth group on Wednesday nights. I still feel bad that they had to endure that, but I could not shake the urge to play music. I even started messing around with a harmonica and let me tell you, you will know what kind of friends you have if they'll put up with you learning how to play a harmonica.

Now, if you lean in close, I will tell you a secret. I used to rap! I would rap for pep-rallys in high school and I would rap at church. In my small circle, that's what I was known for I did a lot of that from the ages of 16 to 21. Just picture me doing the wave while holding a microphone, now that's funny! Rapping was a lot of fun and I really enjoyed it but there was still something missing. I truly felt like there was something else for me musically. By the time I was 22, I had pretty much given up on playing the drums. For the life of me, I just could not get it together! Then (insert super hero music here), the big day finally arrived! I went on a trip to Tybee Island, GA with my youth group. We were going to do some skits and music for a local church. When we got there, we had a little time to kill and they had a drum kit. I decided to try one more time. All I know to say about it is this, a light came down from Heaven and hit me square in the face! I was playing the drums. It wasn't fancy, it wasn't incredible, it was a simple beat and it made sense to me! I couldn't believe it! I was actually playing the drums! I 'remember some friends looking at me with that "When did you start playing drums?" stare. I believe that God taught me how to play drums on that day and He's been teaching me ever since.

The end, not really! The story goes on from there. We returned home from our youth trip to Tybee Island on a Friday and then on Sunday, there was no drummer at church. The service was going to start in 5 minutes and the youth pastor comes to me and says "Hey! I saw you playing drums in Tybee so you should come up here and play." For those of you who don't know, playing a very basic drum beat and playing for a church service are 2 ENTIRELY different things. Especially if you don't want to look like an idiot in front of 150 people!

We argued about it for a couple of minutes and I reluctantly agreed to go up on stage and play. Let me try to paint a picture of this for you. The church drum kit was a basic, entry level drum kit. It had no normal parts to keep the kick drum in place. The solution to that was to put a cement block in front of the kick drum to keep it from sliding forward. It also had a rack tom, floor tom and a snare drum that obviously came with the kit. The drum heads looked like they had been on the drums since the Civil War and they sounded awful.

The last two glorious additions to the drum kit were a hi-hat cymbal and a ride/crash cymbal. It's pretty much a given in the world of drumming that any ride/crash cymbal will sound horrible by default. This one was no exception! I did my best and I am my own worst critic so I'll be the first to tell you that it did not go well at all, but it was a start. It was the beginning of a new chapter in my life. After the first church service fiasco, I decided that I better start practicing and practicing a lot, constantly, on a regular basis. I did not have my own drums at the time but the drummer for the youth band had just gotten new drums and he was gracious enough to let me play them. I would stay after church on Sundays, I would stay after church on Wednesdays. I would beg friends to let me sit and watch their band rehearsals and I would ask a million questions and get advice from any drummer I knew. I practiced for hours at a time and God was there every step of the way, helping me to soak it all in.

About a year after I started playing, I was able to buy my first drum kit. It was a used kit and I had to put it on lay-away to get it. I brought it home and took all the hardware off the drums. I took all the duct tape off of them, cleaned them thoroughly and put new drumheads on. It sounded great and I was so proud of it! My mom let me set up the drums in the house and she never cared how long I practiced or what time I practiced.

She did care, however, that her 23 year old son had not gone to college and really didn't want to go because he wanted to be a musician. My dad also shared this sentiment and so, between the 2 of them, they talked me into trying college. That lasted about 5 minutes because I felt that school was getting in the way of playing music. They were both persistent in trying to get me to go back. I know it disappointed both of them and that never makes anyone feel warm and fuzzy but I just couldn't finish school. I had to play music! If I had to go back and do it over, I would have tried to get through school while playing music but hindsight doesn't need glasses, does it?

By the time I quit college, I was in a band with some friends and I had made a major decision, other than the one about leaving school. I decided that, if I was going to be serious about drumming, I would only play music with the purpose of doing God's work. He gave me the gift in the first place, so the least I could do was use that gift for Him. I also decided that I would play with anybody, anywhere at anytime because I needed the experience. If it was for God, I was there! I played in church, in a band, with other bands and eventually with the youth band. I was having a blast learning and playing drums for God but I didn't under-stand the bigger picture, not yet anyway.

Well, playing in the youth band led to, you guessed it, the

extraordinary youth service! It was an experience like I'd never had before. There I was, sitting at the drums, unable to do anything but weep. I truly felt loved and important and that night, God spoke to me. He said this, "Andy, I've called you to preach..." I immediately started to argue with Him. Thoughts like, I can't do that, I'm no speaker, I'm bald, you know, the usual stuff we tell God to get out of doing something. Then He said "Wait. I've called you to preach and this is your pulpit." I didn't know what to do with that. I'd never heard anything like that before but I knew God wasn't really the conventional type.

By faith, I grabbed hold of His words and held tight! As soon as He said them, I knew what they meant. I thought I might be a little crazy, but I knew what they meant. When I left the youth service that night, I left with purpose. I felt renewed, I felt whole and I knew what I was supposed to do! God had called me to play drums and I did! I played with a little extra something from that moment on and it was more fun than ever! There was only 1 small problem. Mom and Dad weren't thrilled by the whole musician thing.

Don't get me wrong, they supported me playing drums, but they also knew how hard it was to make a living at it. They really wanted me to go to school and find a career. Pretty much what any good parent would want for their kids. I fought with that for about 8 years. I had job after job after job after job and I still had no real desire to go to school. All I knew to do was to keep playing drums. About 3 years after the awesome youth service, I really started getting tired of not playing drums for a living. The whole 9 to 5, blue collar job thing was wearing on me. How could God call me to do this awesome thing and here I am stuck at a dead end job.

During that time, there are TWO major things that I remember God showing me. Here is the first. Even though I was at a dead end job, there were people there that needed encouraging and people that needed God's love. What if I was the only picture of God that those people would ever see? When God hits you with something like that, you start to see the bigger picture. The second thing He showed me is this... We need to speak life into our circumstances.

Proverbs 18:21 says "The tongue has the power of life and death, and those who love it will eat it's fruit." I'm not a part of the Name it and claim it crowd, but I do believe what the Bible says and I don't believe it can possibly be harmful to speak positively. So, here's what I did. Whenever someone would ask me what I was doing, I would tell them "I'm a musician, but I deliver office supplies to make money." I'll come back to that one in a few minutes.

Fast forward a couple of years. Lo and behold, God sends me a wonderful, supportive wife who has an amazing singing voice and loves music as much as I do! God is just good like that! We end up living in McDonough, GA and she gets involved with the music at church and I'm still playing drums with 'everybody and all of a sudden. The Lord wanted me to lay off the drumming.

That was a shock! I really didn't understand it but I let go of all drumming responsibilities except for playing in church. The bummer was, my church had just gotten the cheapest set of electric drums they could find. Those things were awful to play! I'm pretty sure that God had some humility for me in all of that. So, there we were. No band. Just church. I had played in bands for about 9 years at that point and I didn't know how to NOT play with some kind of band. That went on for about 6 months when I got a phone call. It was the assistant Music Minister from Eagle's Landing First Baptist Church... in McDonough, GA.

He said "Hey Andy. I've heard you play drums at some different events and I think you'd be good for the youth praise band here at church. They're called Casting Crowns." At that time, CC was not signed or on the road. They were simply playing for the youth at church. I didn't know who they were and I had never said no to anything, so I decided to check it out. I went and played with them here and there but I wasn't totally on board. I almost said no but I prayed about it. A lot. I felt like the Lord was telling me to hang in there because He had something in mind. At this point, if I haven't learned to listen to God, then I had severe issues.

So I decided to trust and obey. I said yes to Casting Crowns and 3 months later, CC was signed to a record contract, which had nothing to do with me. That's the way that God timed it. He's really good at that. We were able to do amazing things in CC like travel around the world and see orphans in Africa. We were able to go to The 50th Annual

Grammy Awards, The GMA Awards and meet celebrities like Albert Pujols.

We were in lavish hotels and we've gone 2 days without a shower. It was an amazing, crazy roller coaster ride and the coolest part of it all was doing it to advance the kingdom of God. It was amazing to watch the Lord work through that band! But that, like all chapters, came to an end.

Toward the end of my time with Casting Crowns, I had formed another band. At first, it was out of necessity because people would ask me to come speak at their church and bring a band. There was no way for CC to be everywhere at one time so I grabbed my wife and some friends and we would play worship for some Fellowship of Christian Athletes events.

We didn't even have a name but it wasn't long until I made everyone choose a name. There was no way we were going to be called the Andy Williams Praise Band. They decided on the name Soul Sister Sally and it stuck. As time went on, God began giving my wife songs to write and we started playing them along with praise and worship tunes. It wasn't long until the band that started off as a fun thing began to get a little more serious. We were seeing God do some very cool things!

I fought it for a while but then I knew. I can't really explain it, I just knew. I was concerned about what my wife, Kelly, would think. When I talked to her about it, she was already on the same page. God had spoken to her as well. It was then time to talk with Casting Crowns about Soul Sister Sally and CC and I lovingly decided to part ways. No one was angry. There were no bitter feelings. God had called me to something else, it is as simple as that.

I am now in music ministry with my wife as Soul Sister Sally and I often think how cool it is to be in a band with her! When the Bible says that a husband and wife are one, there is power in that! A strong husband and wife can be a force to be reckoned with. Why do you think the enemy is so concerned with destroying marriages and families? When I left CC, people told me that I was crazy. People wondered how I could make it musically by leaving CC.

Here's what those people didn't understand. Man is not my provider. God, alone, is my provider. It hasn't 'been the easiest road but the road to obedience never is. The road to the cross was horrible for Jesus but He was obedient. It wasn't easy for me to tell people "I'm a musician, but I deliver office supplies to make money." I felt stupid doing that and look what happened, something amazing!

I thought it was crazy when God asked me to quit playing drums with the exception of a sorry electronic drum kit at church. I was completely bummed out over that one! I spent 8 years of my life feeling like a complete loser because I wasn't doing exactly what people thought I should do and you know what? It's ok. It truly is ok because I did what I felt like God wanted me to do. How can the one who created us, steer us wrong? He can't. It's not in His nature. A friend of mine asked me recently "Can we have faith in God, yet not fully trust Him?" When we trust God fully, when we are willing to literally put our lives in His hands, we can see unbelievable things happen! I don't know if you are nearing the end of a chapter in your life or beginning a new one but please know this. God loves you! He formed you in your mother's womb. He knows the number of hairs on your head, or lack thereof.

Jeremiah 29:11 - **"For I know the plans I have for you, declares the Lord, plans to prosper you and not to harm you, plans to give you hope and a future."** God may be calling to you to something you think is purely outrageous. You might be scared to death to take that leap of faith. Your friends might even think you're a fry short of a happy meal. It may not be the easiest thing you've ever done but He WILL catch you. Just close your eyes and jump!

Chapter Six

"Broken but Blessed"

TAMMY WALLACE – CANTON, GA

Tammy Wallace is a lifelong resident of Canton, Georgia. She was married to Creig Wallace for 21 years before he went home to be with the Lord. She has 2 beautiful children; Hannah is 17 and Andrew is 13. Our daughter Hope is in heaven with her Dad. Tammy is the operations manager/ owner of The Carpenter's Shop Christian Preschool. They are active members at Woodstock First Baptist Church www.FBCW.org and have the absolute best pastor in the world – Dr Johnny Hunt. Tammy feels truly blessed by God and can't wait to see what He has in store for our future! For bookings call 770-720-2333 or twallace.thecarpentershop@hotmail.com

**

MY mind just couldn't seem to absorb the words she was telling me. No one can ever get ready to hear these words. We thought we were only here to find out if treatment for Creig's cancer would be continuing. Now the Physician's assistant was telling me that there was nothing more that could be done for Creig. Not only would he not be continuing treatment but it appeared that his body was shutting down. They could only make him comfortable and let things happen naturally. It was two days before Thanksgiving and she hoped the fluids he was getting would allow him to make it through the weekend.

The journey had only begun 7 months earlier. Creig had a cough that just wouldn't go away. After seeing the Dr. and two rounds of anti-biotics a scan was ordered. The scan showed a large tumor on his right kidney and it had metastasized to his lungs. When the Dr. left the room to get an appointment with an oncologist, Creig looked at and said "I am sorry you have to go through this." To which I replied "Everything I have gone through in life has been to prepare me for this moment." We both knew at that moment that our hope relied in God and God alone. We began in that office at that moment seeking direction and trusting Him completely.

As we left the Drs. office our thoughts turned to our children. Hannah was now 12 years old; she and her Dad had always been close. Andrew was 8 years old; he was always full of questions. Our first thoughts were to be completely honest and answer all of their questions to the best of our abilities. It was in those moments that we felt as if God had prepared their hearts and had given us the words to say. It is in those deepest darkest times in life that I feel the closest to God. I have heard it said that "we are either in a storm in our life"; "entering a storm in our life"; or "coming out of a storm in our life". I don't think you can find anyone that would volunteer to have a "storm". Creig and I had been married for 22 years when he was diagnosed and in those years we had always faced our "storms" by trusting in God.

We had faced 5 years of infertility before becoming pregnant with our first child. We had found out at our 20 week sonogram of our 2nd child that she had some severe abnormalities and would not live once she was born. The Dr. advised us that we could abort the pregnancy if we wanted. Creig and I both agreed that we would not end the pregnancy.

God had given this baby life and we would not be the ones to end it. I could feel the baby moving and tried to enjoy this time as much as possible. It was during this time that I first experienced praying to God for something and having peace that it would be okay, but never had peace that our baby would live. We decided to name our baby girl Hope Delaine, Delaine was her Dad's middle name. Hope was because we put our hope in God. She only lived for 45 minutes. We would comfort one another by saying that we only got to hold her for 45 minutes on earth but we would get to hold her an eternity. My Dad passed away the same year from a brain tumor. We faced all of these trials with prayer and trust.

Creig had surgery to remove his kidney and the tumor. He exceeded the Dr.'s expectations. The oncologist had explained that the only way to achieve remission with this type of cancer was for Creig to receive a high dose medication called IL2. He would need to go through a lung function test to see if that would be possible. It was determined that his lung where not strong enough due to the presence of the cancer. He would be starting an oral medication called Sutent. He would take this for two weeks followed by one week off. This medication left him with mouth sores, nausea and weakness. After two rounds he had a scan to see if there was any change in the tumors in his lungs. There was no change, but the scan showed fluid around his heart. An echo test was done on his heart and it was determined that his heart was not damaged from the fluid. His blood count had dropped to six and his calcium levels were dangerously high. Creig was given a blood transfusion and treatment for the high levels of calcium. The Dr. decided that the Sutent was causing too many other health problems to continue treatment. Creig started another oral medication called Nexavar. After just two days on this medication he developed a high fever that sent us to the ER. After a week stay at the hospital he was put on a drug called Torisel. This would be given once a week and injected through an IV.

At this point it had only been six months since Creig's diagnoses. He had lost 100 pounds and could only tolerate a protein drink called boost. He was on oxygen continuously, he had nose bleeds. Horrible nausea and vomiting that was with him daily. In all of this Creig never complained. He was the best patient you could ask for. He stayed positive and encouraged everyone he came into contact with. Creig's theme song became "Praise you in the Storm" by Casting Crowns.

We were blessed to be surrounded by many friends and family that were prayer warriors. We could feel the prayers and knew that God would supply our every need. There were times when I would be concerned or worried about something, I would pray about it before going to bed and by the next morning that worry would be gone from my memory.

Our weekly trips to Emory continued without much change. I began to dread Creig getting on the scale, his weight continued to drop weekly. He was now riding in a wheelchair when he left the house. His only outings were going to Emory for treatment or Drs. Appointments. Still his positive attitude was amazing. After about eight weeks of Torisel treatments on one of our regular check-ins it was determined that Creig's oxygen level was low and he was admitted to the hospital to see if the drug was working against him. A scan was performed and it was determined that the treatment was actually shrinking the tumors. PRAISE GOD!!

Finally, something positive. Although the Dr. had told us that this drug would not put the cancer in remission we knew that we served a God of miracles and that He could chose to heal him at any time. Every hospital stay seemed to take a toll on all of us. Creig would come home weaker and the children were having trouble dealing with our absence. It was during this stay that the recommendation of our team of Drs. and much prayer we decided to enlist the help of hospice. The nurses could make weekly trips to monitor Creig's condition, which was a great comfort to me and would help catch little problems that could be corrected before a hospital stay was necessary.

Creig told one of the nurses that he allowed them to come because he thought it would help me. It had been his wish to keep things as normal as possible for the kids, so I continued to work and take them to their functions. Creig always put our needs before his and still maintained his positive attitude. He never talked about death or dying; it was as if that would have been giving the cancer an edge on him, giving up some hope that we needed to hang onto. Maybe he just thought he was protecting me.

Our weekly trips to Emory continued for another month without much change. Until Creig's blood work revealed that his Creatinine levels were high. High Creatinine levels could cause kidney failure, Creig only having one kidney this would be dangerous. This was the only treatment that had showed any shrinkage in the tumors and now it could be causing the Creatinine levels to rise. The Dr. asked us to come back in a week for more blood work to see if this was the case. He explained if this was found to be the case we would have to make a decision on whether to continue treatment or discontinue it.

If we discontinued it we would go home with managed hospice care, if we continued it with high Creatine levels it could damage his only kidney and put him into kidney failure. Creig continued to lose even more weight, he now weighed less than I did and he was six feet tall. The kids were having a hard time watching their Dads health decline so drastically. We still did not give up; we knew that we served a God that had the power to heal. Our lives rested in His hands and we were leaning on Him for our every need.

As my mind tried to focus on her words my heart was breaking. I knew that what we were about to face was going to be the most difficult time of our lives. With God's help I knew I could get through this. But my kids, just the thought of them losing their Dad at such a young age was more than I could stand at that moment. As I entered the room where Creig was receiving fluids he asked what the Dr. had told me. I just simply told him that they were not going to be able to continue his treatment, so we would not be returning to Emory anymore. I stopped there; I could not bring myself to tell him that he was dying. Creig has been such an inspiration to me through this journey. He never gave up hope and to tell him would be taking some of that hope away and I couldn't do that.

Creig had become so weak that he could not walk about the house any longer.

The hospice nurse suggested that we get a hospital bed for him that would allow him to stay in the family room. Creig agreed to that reluctantly. He was so independent and he wanted things to continue as normal as possible. He asked me if I could contact a nursing home to drop him off during the day so I could continue to work. I just smiled and told him that would not be necessary, I would be taking care of him. I prayed and tried to prepare to break the news to my children. We went for a ride and as gently as I could I told them that God was going to have to take their Dad to heaven to heal him. That the Drs. had told me that there was nothing more they could do for him. They both broke down and we all cried together. It hurt to see them in so much pain.

Andrew asks me a day or so later if God could heal his Dad if He wanted to. I told him yes, but it looked as if He would have to take him to heaven to do that. To which he replied, but He could heal him on earth couldn't He? Yes He could, Andrew never gave up believing that God could perform a miracle and heal his Dad. Andrew told me, "I don't think this is fair. To which I replied "Life isn't fair. We are not called to be Christians because it is easy. We are called to be Christians to point others to God. That is what your Dad did every day of his life." We had always prayed that God's will be done in this journey and it appeared that God's will was going to be to take Creig to heaven.

Creig remained very alert but grew weaker by the day. Creig told me he would not wish this on his worst enemy and he was sorry that I had to go through this. I told him it was an honor and a privilege to care for him. This is what the marriage vows mean when it says "for better or worse, in sickness or in health". Creig and I had been married for 22 years and God had granted us many good things in our marriage. Family and friends were in and out of the house for the next couple of days. By late Saturday Creig was too weak to talk. He still knew what was going on around him and knew who we were. Family took Hannah and Andrew to the movies to get them out for the house of a little while. As the evening went on Creig became more and more restless. We were surrounded with friends and my mom was there.

Someone put on the cd Precious Memories by Alan Jackson. It was then I pulled my chair up close to his bed and laid my head on the bed rail and began to pray. The third song on the cd was "I will fly away", that was one of Creig's favorites. When I looked up at Creig when that song began to play he wasn't breathing. I called his name and he took a breath. It was then that I told him "Hannah, Andrew and I will be ok. It is ok if you need to go. I told him to hold Hope until I got there." He took one more breath and he was gone. Creig had been healed! He was now in the presence of Jesus and had a new body free from cancer. Cancer took away a lot, but it didn't take away his spirit, his will to live or desire to witness for his Savior.

I was glad for Creig but my heart was broken. We had become one when we married and I felt as if a part of me had been ripped apart. Now I had to break the news to my children. They had not spent the night at home. I had decided at God's urging that they didn't need to be at home that night. Surrounded by friends and family I broke the news to them. I simply told them that their Dad had gone home to be with Jesus. We all sobbed together. My heart broke all over again. It hurts to see your children in so much pain. At that moment I could see all the things that Creig would miss in their lives and all the things Hannah and Andrew would accomplish and their Dad would not be there to see it. Plans were made for Creig's visitation and his funeral. Creig had so many wonderful friends that wanted to come pay their respects. I received one of the greatest complements from one of those friends. She told me that Creig was the greatest Christian she had ever known. I thought that spoke volumes about Creig and his character. Creig's job was the facility supervisor for our church. Although he wasn't a minister he used his job to minister to those around him. Most of which was done behind the scenes. That was Creig he was always a behind the scenes kind of guy.

The funeral was exactly what I thought Creig would have wanted. The songs sung were his favorites, the men that spoke knew him well. Now we had to start living our lives without Creig. That would be the hardest part. I knew that the grief process was painful, but it was a journey that had to be taken. It wasn't something that you could ignore. I also knew that with God's help we would get through it. I found myself in a role I had never thought about. I was now a "single mom" and a "widow". I was now the head of the household. Creig was always the spiritual leader in our house. He was also our "voice of reason".

Creig had the joy of leading both of our children to the Lord. Now just the thought of that brings me so much peace. That one day our family will be reunited in heaven. Creig had taught Sunday School all of our married lives and nothing thrilled him more than to see a child accept Jesus as their Savior. He had a special place in his heart for children and him in theirs.

See, I am doing a new thing! I am making a way in the desert and streams in the wasteland. Isa. 43:19

I found this to be so true. God was truly doing "a new thing" in our lives. God had provided for our every need and allowed so many wonderful people to come into our lives. That is "making a way in the desert and streams in the wasteland." One of my greatest joys was seeing both Hannah and Andrew realize that God was at work in their lives. Hannah had prayed specifically for guidance in what she should do concerning the upcoming school year.

Hannah was in middle school when Creig was diagnosed and after his death she had such a hard time in school that she had returned to a private school she had attended earlier in her school career. I felt that she would benefit from returning there for the 8th grade instead of moving on to high school. But I also felt she needed to have input in this decision. She did pray and come to the conclusion that she should return to repeat the 8th grade. It was then that I realized that I am not alone in this. God is father to the fatherless and husband to the husbandless. None of this had caught God by surprise; He knew what lay ahead of us and had gone on before us making a way for us to get through this. All we had to do was ask Him to show us His will for our lives and then follow it.

Some of the deepest and greatest conversations came from Andrew. Just when I thought I was going to say something to help him in his journey he would say something to help me in mine. Now that has to be God at work. He told me in one conversation "You know Mom the cancer didn't win, it lost. When Dad died it died.

God defeated it; He won because Dad is with Him now. I hate cancer". Wow; what insight for a 9 year old. That could only come from God. Some of our best conversations would come when we were driving down the road. One such conversation started when Andrew and I were discussing the men God had placed in his life both before and after Creig's death. He named 5 men that he feels has had an impact in his life. I shared with him that God says in the Bible that "I will be husband to the husbandless and father to the fatherless."

Andrew immediately said "Oh I get it God took my Dad but He placed these men in my life to help me since I don't have my Dad." At that moment I was glad that he was setting behind me so he couldn't see the tears in my eyes. I am so proud of my children for allowing God to work in their lives. God is working behind the scenes every day in our lives. Now that 4 years has past and some of these men are no longer in Andrew's life. I find myself getting a little sad because I know how much Andrew needs Godly mentors in his life. I realize that people get busy and have their own families and find no fault with these men. But as soon as I prayed about my concern to God, He brought someone else into his life. Often God will provide a way before I even know that I needed a way.

But you, O Lord are a shield for me, My glory and the One who lifts my head. Psalms 3:3

Many times through that first year I knew that God had been my shield. He had protected me in ways that I am aware of and ways that I was not. He was the One who lifted my head with His gentle embrace. I had become so aware of God's presence in my life. I know if it was not for Him I would not be where I am today. My life forever changed when Creig died. I am not the same person that I was before. It was as if my life had been pressed through a sifter.

The unimportant things fell away and the important things held together. My world seems to be more black and white and have less gray in it. One of the things I miss most about Creig is his leadership role as the head of our house. I miss talking with him and getting his input on decisions that must be made. I also miss his sense of humor. But most of all I miss him being here as a Dad. Hannah, Andrew and I talk about Creig on a regular basis. We share a memory, laugh at something he did or said. That is our way of keeping his memory alive in our hearts.

"I will not die but live, and will proclaim what the LORD has done." Ps. 118:17

Have you ever tried to let go of something and hold on to it at the same time? The grieving process is like that. As I make my way through the journey I look backward to see how far I have come. As I look forward it is hard to look too far into the future because it is hard to think of facing the major events in our lives without Creig being there. I know that we will have Creig's memory in our hearts and nothing can ever take that away. I know that the pain will lessen as time passes but we will never stop missing him. I know that I must find the best way for us to move through this journey. First and foremost is to allow God to direct my path.

We made it through all "the first". Some were harder than others.

Some I expected to be difficult, others caught me by surprise. As we approached the second anniversary of Creig's death I was at a routine Drs. Appointment when my breast specialist ordered a MRI to get a better look at a cyst in my breast. I was prone to have cyst, so this was not a big concern for me. I prayed for God's will to be done, but knew the reality was that I might not like His will for my life. The Dr. called and asked for me to come in so they could check my incision sites, but when I got there she used the ultra sound to look at something else. It was at that moment I knew that the lump I had felt and MRI biopsy had found was something more. Once again I heard those words, "we know what it is and it is bad news".

She asked if I had brought my friend and if I want to get her so she could explain what they had found. She explained that I had breast cancer. It was at least a stage I(invasive ductal carcinoma) , I had two lumps in my right breast. I was not a candidate for a lumpectomy because I have more than one. My Dr. recommended that I have a double mastectomy. The left would be removed for precautionary reasons. She was pretty certain that is had not spread to the lymph nodes. I had a PET scan before surgery to be certain.

Again my first thoughts went to my children. Their only knowledge of cancer was what they experienced with their Dad. If I told them I had cancer they would think I was going to die too. As I told family and friends I asked them not to tell the kids, until I had decided the best way to handle it. I began to pray and ask God to prepare their hearts. I knew He could protect them even when I couldn't.

Those who know your name will trust in you, for you, LORD, have never forsaken those who seek you. Psalm 9:10

Within a week I found out that Hannah had requested prayer for me at Sunday School. She had told them that her Mom had cancer. I then talked with her and explained what was going on and we decided it was best not to tell Andrew. It was then I realized how much she had matured since her Dad had died. I had my PET scan and it appeared that the cancer was localized. A surgery date was set. I had been telling

Andrew up to this point that I was going to have some surgery to remove some spots and I would need to stay in the hospital for a couple of days.

Once I told him when I would be having surgery he asked where the spots were located. After I told him, he looked straight at me and said "do you have breast cancer?" That was Andrew, always just wanted the facts. I told him yes. But the Dr. thought they could remove all the cancer with surgery. I had a test called centennial lymph node test right before surgery. This was done by putting dye in the lymph system and it would show the Drs. where the centennial lymph node was located. This would allow them to only remove the nodes that was affected by the cancer and not have to remove all or large amounts of nodes. I had a double mastectomy with immediate reconstruction. That means that all my breast tissue was removed and expanders were placed during surgery.

When I woke in my room my first question was "Was any lymph nodes involved?" The answer was "Yes, three." At that moment I had a peace that only God can give about the lymph nodes that were involved. We would have to wait on a pathology report to be sure how involved it was. I stayed in the hospital for two days. I came home with 4 drains, 2 on each side. I could not lift my hands above my head. This was hard for me because I was used to being the one doing the care taking, not the one being cared for. It was during this time that I had many wonderful family and friends come to my rescue in the way of meals, calls, cards, anything I needed doing.

I don't see how anyone who doesn't have a church family can make it through a difficult time. Mine has come to my rescue many times. Andrew's first question was "did they remove all the cancer." I told him "yes" but I would have to have some treatments to make sure that they killed all the cancer cells. After the drains were removed the reconstructive process started. I would go in the plastic surgeon once a week and he would inject saline solution into the expanders; this was done to stretch the skin in preparation for the implants.

When I returned to my surgeon for a post op appointment she had received my pathology report. I had only had cancer in two lymph nodes. This was great news because with two you don't have to have radiation. Now I just had to go see the oncologist for a game plan. My first appointment with my oncologist went well. I was amazed at how much knowledge this Dr. had about cancer, cancer studies and treatment. It was hard to try to absorb all the information she was giving me. It was determined that my breast cancer was a stage 2 and I would need to have 6 chemo treatments. I would be given one treatment every three weeks. My surgeon would place my port on my birthday and I would start chemo the day after. My reconstruction was put on hold until I finished my treatments. All my plans were made. I had selected a wig and had even found a hat that had a strip of hair Velcro into it, and this was great for those casual days when you didn't want to wear a wig.

The chemo treatments consisted of 3 different drugs. I would have to return the following day for an injection. Steroids were given a few days before to try and help with nausea. I am sure many studies, trials and treatments went into the combination of drugs. As I sat there receiving my first chemo treatment I couldn't help but think of Creig and how many times I sat beside him to receive his treatments. The infusion lab where I received treatment was much warmer and less sterile than the lab where Creig received his treatment. The side effects started soon after the first treatment. Nausea was the first side effect to rear its ugly head. I had been given oral meds to try and help with this. Then it became difficult to swallow. All foods seemed dry and even liquids had to be forced down. On day 3 I started to have migraines, those were followed by body aches and soreness. By day 5 I was plagued with fatigue. The type of fatigue that it doesn't matter how much you rest it doesn't go away. Then as quickly as the side effects came they would be gone. I would return to work and try to get back to normal as quickly as possible. I tried not to think of how many days till my next treatment, but tried to concentrate on how many good days I had. I didn't dread the side effects until they came, I thought that would be wasting some of the good time that I had between treatments.

When I had selected my wig they had told me that my hair would probably fall out after the second treatment, but call them if it started earlier and I could come in for my fitting. Well it started to let go after two weeks. It wasn't just falling out, but if you reached up and pulled it then it would come out in your hand. I went in and had them shave my hair down to a ¼ inch. I thought this was fitting since it was Creig's birthday. When Creig's hair stated to thin we just kept it buzzed. Now I had a Creig haircut in honor of him on his birthday. Within a few days all of my hair let go.

After the second treatment the Dr. changed my nausea meds and that seemed to help with the nausea as well as the migraines. The nausea was still there, but I was able to keep something on my stomach which made it more tolerable. I still had low-grade migraines, fatigue and muscle aches for about five days. The Dr. also decided that I might need some fluids on day 3. It was determined that I was becoming dehydrated after a couple of days and this could be causing the migraines. Returning to the infusion lab when I felt so bad was not something I wanted to do, but if it would help with some of the side effects then I would do it. Getting fluids did help so it was determined that I would do this after each treatment.

Andrew was my helper and nurse after I would have a chemo treatment. I heard him tell someone that I didn't have those bad headaches this time. I think that really bothered him the first time that happened. Hannah was also a big help during the chemo treatments she had gotten her learners permit and would be my chauffer during treatment weeks. One of the drugs in my regimen caused my hair to fall out, retain fluid and have "chemo brain". The hair falling out didn't bother me; I knew it would come back once I was finished. The fluid had caused me to gain weight and had settled in my right arm because of the lymph nodes that were removed.

The Dr. sent me to a therapist that specialized in lymphedema, she thought it was temporary and could be treated with wrapping and some therapy. As for the "chemo brain" it was temporary too. It is the most frustrating because it probably affected my day to day life the most. It can cause a "fog" like effect, along with a problem with recall and some short term memory loss. I asked Andrew to help me to remember something to which he replied "Mom you need to write it down, you know I will not remember and you have that "chemo brain" thing going on." The chemo weeks were spent dealing with the side effects and the two weeks in between were spent trying to remember what I am supposed to be doing. I received my 6th and final treatment on April 21st one day after what would have been my 24th wedding anniversary. Someone said

"That has gone by really quickly." Well....that depends. The chemo weeks go by slowly and the non-chemo weeks go by fast. The side effects had become predictable in order but not in severity.

It always seemed that one side effect last longer or was more severe than usual. One side effect that came during the last few treatments was a feeling like acid reflux. I would take some over the counter drugs to help with this. Some of the side effects that I experienced I had never experienced before and therefore could not identify with someone who had them. After chemo I had a better understanding and could be sympathetic with someone who had a bout with one of these side effects. It was during my first round of chemo and side effects that Creig became my hero. When I was feeling my worst I couldn't help but think about how much Creig had gone through. He was so sick for months. My worst side effects only lasted for a few days.

Creig never complained and would tell anyone who asked him that he wasn't in any pain. Once again I could see God working in our lives. The kids could see our lives return to normal after a week of treatment. We would have two weeks of normal for us before a week of treatment. They never got to see their Dad do this. Once he was diagnosed he gradually got worse for seven months. I had several more outpatient surgeries for the reconstruction process. Each one was "a piece of cake" compared to the mastectomy surgery.

It took 20 months for diagnoses to finished reconstruction. It was determined that the cancer is fed by estrogen so I am taking a chemo pill called tamoxifen. By removing all estrogen from my body it will send me into menopause. The most common side effect is hot flashes. I should have to take this for 3-5 years. I can't help but feel so blessed to have made it through this journey. Because of the early diagnoses the cancer was removed and the treatment was tolerable. Would I choose to go through this again; absolutely not? Will I use this experience to glorify God and help other who are going through the same thing? Every chance I get!

I believe one of the reasons God allowed this in my life was so my children could see that God can heal on earth. In the case of their Dad God had to take him to heaven to heal him. I have had friends say "I don't know how you do this." To which I reply "It is all God." I am here to tell you it doesn't matter what you are going through. God will help you through it, if you only allow him to do so. When you can't follow His hand, trust His heart!

THE WEAVER

My life is but a weaving
Between my Lord and me,
I cannot choose the colors
He worketh steadily.

Oftimes He weaveth sorrow,
And I in foolish pride
Forget He sees the upper
And I, the underside.

Not till the loom in silent
And the shuttles cease to fly
Shall God unroll the canvas
And explain the reason why.

The dark threads are as needful
In the Weaver's skillful hand
As the threads of gold and silver
In the pattern He has planned.

- Author Unknown

I have thought of this poem often. I think it says it "all". We don't always understand why God allows the things that happen in our lives. It is not ours to understand, nor does He owe us an explanation for it. Even if He chose to tell us the "why", would it be enough? It wouldn't change anything. When we get to heaven that is when He will unroll the canvas. Then we will see the fabric of our lives and we will see it from His point of view. We will see the dark threads of sorrow and the brighter threads of gold and silver.

What looked like a knotted mess from our point of few will be a masterpiece that only the Master can weave. I thought Randy Pausch said it best when he said "We cannot change the cards we are dealt, just how we play the hand." We would never choose the dark threads to enter our lives. When they do we must choose how we react to them. That is where I am in this journey of my life.

I cannot change what has happened in our lives. I can only do my best to help my children understand that God can help them through this difficult time and He can use it to allow them to help others. I tell them often "God must think they are very special that they can handle this in their lives at such a young age and He must have something big planned for their lives." As I think of where I have been, what I have come through and where I am going. I know there is no doubt that I would not have made it this far if it were not for God in my life. He has been there to guide and direct my path through this journey.

Chapter Seven

"Standing Tall – After the Fall"

DR. TIM LEE – GARLAND, TX
www.TimLee.org

Dr Tim Lee is a national treasure. Having lost both legs in Vietnam with the U.S. Marines Corps in 1971 after stepping on a grenade God has been using him ever since traveling the globe with the glorious Gospel. For over four decades Evangelist Tim Lee has been serving in the Lord's Army and considered by many church leaders to be one of the greatest evangelists of modern times. He is passionate, patriotic and powerful in the pulpit.

Brother Tim has preached in some of America's largest churches and the local country church while holding crusades in various nations. Tim is also the host of the annual "Youth Alive" teen camp where literally thousands of young people have made eternal commitments to Christ and scores called into full-time ministry. Evangelist Tim Lee is a prophet bringing back America to God. He has served on the Board at Liberty University in Lynchburg, VA for 20 yrs and Tim has ministered to U.S. Presidents and people of every race, color and class. Tim is married to his lovely wife, Connie and they have three children and six grand-children. If you want a visit from Heaven book Dr Tim Lee today! You can follow Tim on Twitter @MarineTimLee

I Samuel 2:4 *"The bows of the mighty men are broken, and they that stumbled are girded with strength."* Henri Nouwen wrote in his book, *The Return of the Prodigal Son*, that "it is often difficult to believe that there is much to think, speak or write about other than brokenness".

Mark Buchanan wrote in his book *Your God is Too Safe*, that there is one soil that usually withers pride—It is brokenness. "But all these things keep him low, mar his pride, crush his self-righteousness, cut the locks of his presumption, stain his self conceit, stop his boasting, preserve him from despising others, make him take the lowest room, teach him to esteem others better than himself, drive him to earnest prayer, fit him as an object of mercy, break to pieces his free will, and lay him low at the feet of the Redeemer, as one to be saved by sovereign grace alone!" —author unknown

It is March of 2011. As I sit in my office in the Dallas metro-plex, I look out the window to the horizon. It has been a good journey. I think back to the turbulent sixties and find there a very troubled young man; an angry Junior High school student standing defiantly under the secrecy of a concrete bridge in McLeansboro, Illinois, just across the street from his school. It is 1964. He is peering out from under his multi-ton cover looking for any familiar cars or pick-up trucks with passengers that might report his doings. Slowly he takes several long draws off a Marlboro cigarette, with closed eyes, blowing the smoke up into the damp air. He doesn't want to be caught committing this forbidden act, yet it really doesn't matter to him if he is. He is at war with the whole raging world and really doesn't give a care who doesn't like it.

We move ahead to 1969. Bobby Kennedy and Martin Luther King, Jr. are dead. Led Zeppelin will soon rock the youth culture. Elvis will make a comeback with *"Long Black Limousine"*. A teenager known as "Robert R." will die in nearby St. Louis, Missouri, of a mysterious disease, which, in 1984, will be confirmed as the first case of HIV/AIDS in North America. Woodstock will rage, and two Black Panthers will be shot dead in their sleep by Chicago police officers. Charles Manson will conduct his murderous vendetta in

California, America will successfully land a man on the moor and "return him safely to the earth." Nixon will take office, *Butch Cassidy and the Sundance Kid* will heat up the big screen and the Beatles will take the world by storm. The young man's world is spinning faster and faster; it will approach warp speed. Dave Thomas will open Wendy's, Wal Mart will shake the marketing world, the astonishing Mets will win the World Series and Broadway Joe Namath's mouth and throwing arm will tame the mighty Colts in Super Bowl III. Yasser Arafat will come to power in the Mideast, the Boeing 747 will make its maiden flight and *Midnight Cowboy*, an X-rated, Oscar winning film will shock the American public and remove the blinders from the eyes of millions of youth and young adults. And, half-a-world-away, in the jungles of a 3rd world nation called Vietnam, a place most Americans could not find on a map, American boys are killing and being killed.

That was my world—at least the outside world. I was disconnected from it all. As I look at this kid now, this was a truly angry young man. An arc of rebellion eats at his belly. He is becoming hell in the flesh. He is the son of a preacher and has recoiled at the expectations of people that he follow his father's call. That animosity has driven him relentlessly to rebellion. To make money he steals seven brand new air-conditioning units from an appliance store on the square in McLeansboro. He has become well known to the local police. His future is replete with bar fights with men twice his size (all of which he is the victor), drag races, nights of drunken misery and carousing, the flashing lights of numerous police cars and a near-death encounter with a semi tractor-trailer that would put him flat on his back for several days in a hospital in Mt Vernon, Illinois. He emerges stiffly, defiantly and more determined than ever to continue his raid on madness and anarchy.

Though he is a stellar athlete and his picture regularly appears in the local county papers for his accomplishments (two of them records that would stand for a quarter century) in the football, baseball and basketball arenas—nothing really directs his life other than his self-worship and an innate desire to drive on in his berserk/frenzied self-imposed Armageddon. His family is exhausted, his coaches are perplexed, his preacher-father is out of answers and his saintly mother, suffering from one of his many out-rages during which he screamed at her with such fierceness that she passes out. He is, at this point, out of control, crazily enamored with his own self-powers that are driving him into a destructive future.

Finally, in self desperation, he runs away from home, to crime invested E. St. Louis. He gets a job washing dishes and living in a cheap boarding house. In this dingy under-world environment, he will one night find a .38 revolver pressed to his head and he will come within a mere second of death. After being spotted by a relative he returns home where his mom and dad welcome him with open arms and unconditional love.

"he came to himself..." Luke 15.17

One day he is walking aimlessly down South Jackson Street in McLeansboro. As he passes the Post Office at 211 S. Jackson Street, it is a little past 11:00 AM in the morning. For the first time in a long time, he is dramatically stopped in his tracks—not by a local beauty, not by a hot car, and not by the local hoods, but by a Marine Corps poster and the words that would change his life..."*The Marines are looking for a few good men.*"

The troubled 18-year-old figured that someone had put the poster there on the lawn just for him. He scanned very carefully the squared-jawed expressionless face, the dazzling blue coat, the glimmering gold buttons crested with the eagle and anchor, first appearing in 1804, making them the oldest military insignia in continued use. His eyes are enticed by the white gloves, the stunning cover with its bill pulled down tight to just over the top of two intimidating eyes.

The Marine is holding a glistening Mameluke sword*, originally given to Lieutenant Presley O'Bannon in 1805 by a Mameluke chieftain in North Africa. It is the oldest weapon still in service by United States Armed Forces. Its pointed tip rests firmly on the Marine's chest and right shoulder. The Eagle, Globe and Anchor emblem fires his mind. The square gold buckle uniting the pure white belt arouses new energy in his soul. This was class personified if he had ever seen it. This was a man's man. The was the epitome and essence of the true fighter. He is dazed, held, thunder-struck/silent. All other sounds and impressions are driven from his mind for several long moments as he studies the image before him. Done. He will become a Marine.

Within six months he arrives at Parris Island, South Carolina, to begin his training. Yellow footprints lead him into the presence of the legendary Marine Corps drill instructor. He was then sent to Camp

LeJuene, North Carolina. Though the training is demanding, he excels, winning three meritorious promotions. He attends ITR training and receives his orders for Vietnam in the spring of 1970. His basic training is completed at Camp LeJeune, North Carolina.

The Marines had changed his life. He had learned discipline, respect, order and manliness. His tour in Vietnam had gone very well. He had discovered natural leadership traits. He had quickly won the respect of his men. By March of 1971, he had completed 8 months of his tour of duty. March 8, 1971, arrived just like any normal day. He would take his men out in the field with a detachment of South Korean Marines and conduct mine sweeping operations in Quang Nam Province.

All un-spent mortar rounds and land mines would be cleared from the area. His squad was walking an abandoned road in a desolate section of the province. It was a little after noon. The squad had stopped for C-rations. Corporal Lee Gore had asked permission to walk point that afternoon. The young man felt responsible for the new men in the squad and had informed Gore that he would continue walking point and finish the afternoon. On this day, a well placed 60-pound box mine (a device used to take out tanks) would violently intersect with this young Marine.

The squad had just passed a crumbling Buddhist temple. They were walking next to a field of elephant grass. It was quiet. One last step on the legs that had carried him to a standout high school sports career. One more step on the legs that had provided his great venture away from the will of God. One more step on the legs that had taken his feet off the path of righteousness. One more step, and then a deafening explosion erupted from the ground. "It was", as one of his men would describe it 28 years later "as if someone had poured a 5-gallon bucket of dark red paint all over your body."

Earl Lewis, fifth man in formation—"Lee suddenly disappeared in a black cloud..."

Seconds after the blast...

I could hear virtually nothing. It was like being underwater. The whole visible world was murky, ghostly. All the noise was flat and muffled. It was as if the men were moving and jumping around in slow motion, screaming as with their mouths full of Kleenex. Lee Gore, my best friend in Nam, and one of the few real Christians I had met, is holding me, weeping and praying for God to spare my life. Lee's black face is streaming tears. The guys are ripping out their personal bandages and soaking up the spurting blood from my wounds. Blackness. Numbness. Nothing. Then suddenly back to consciousness. In and out.

The whirling blades of the evac-chopper suddenly whizzed over head. *"Am I dying? Is this death? Is this the end?"* The last face I see is Lee Gore's. The medical books says that "Amputation is the removal of part or all of a body part enclosed by skin. Amputation is derived from the Latin word *'amputare'*, to excise, to cut out. Amputation can occur at an accident site, the scene of an animal attack, or a *battlefield*." — MedicineNet.com

There is a brief flight to the USS Sanctuary. The Sanctuary is officially known as AH-17, a Haven-class hospital ship that is waiting in the gulf of Tokin. Her motto was *"Copiae Servamus"*—We serve the troops. She would win meritorious service from 11 April 1969 to 14 April 1971. Her keel was laid on 28 June, 1944 and commissioned on 20 June, 1945.

She provided highly responsive hospital-ship services to the III Marine Amphibious Force in the Gulf of Tokin. 10,701 times, helicopters landed on her deck bringing in the worst of the wounded and dying civilians, soldiers and Marines. All were welcomed. No one was turned away. In 1971, she is state-of-the-art medical care for wounded Marines. Her surgeons would perform 4,629 major surgical operations and admit 13,500 patients, treating a total of 35,005 servicemen. She could hold 800 patients, 60 officers and a crew of 505. The majority of hostile action wounds were caused by explosive devices, land mines and booby traps.

This is where the story takes an amazing turn. There is a picture in the US Navy Medicine Magazine dated April 1971. It has full length photos of the Sanctuary showing three giant red Crosses painted on her 522' hull: one Cross on the bow, one Cross on the stern and one Cross precisely in the middle of the ship. There is another photo that shows a picture of a chopper landing on her deck. To the right of the picture are the words **"COME UNTO ME."**(Matt 11.28) Sanctuary had three operating rooms aboard—all three rooms where located at ship's mid section—*directly behind the middle Cross!* The rooms were located in this region of the ship to minimize rolling and rocking motion. Tim Lee's world on this day, slowed way down. One leg was left in bloody slivers and chards on the jungle floor, its mangled boot blown to atoms. The other leg, barely attached, according to one eye-witness, pulled free from the body it had helped to carry for 21 years and tumbled from the stretcher falling eerily to the deck of the Sanctuary. The eye-witness had never forgotten the spectacle. The running is over.

This young Marine is helpless, legless, without strength and dying. The ship carried multiple surgeons, two anesthesiologists, a nurse anesthetist and outstanding fully trained operating room technicians. Today, 8 March, 1971, while Ali and Frazier battle in Madison Square Garden, a broken boy, 13,000 miles from home, clings to life. He had run so hard, so very hard and now he had fallen; he had broken. Sanctuary gladly received Sgt Timothy Eldon Lee, the son of Wanda and John Lee of 200 S. Silas Avenue in McLeansboro, Ill. The hospital ship would only be in theatre for 38 more days. CAPT Bryan B. Brown, Jr., USN would soon give orders to lift anchor.

There was room and there was time, just enough time to begin putting the broken boy back together. The glorious picture of the three crosses, today, speaks volumes to my mind and heart. Jesus receives the broken. His Cross not only saves but it mends. (Matt 8.17) He will take all our remaining pieces, put us back on the potter's wheel and remake us! Today, 8 March, 1971, USS Sanctuary was my angel, my ark, my safe house in the arms of God. Maybe an angel whispered to another "This broken boy will one day preach to hundreds of thousands of people. He will shake hands with Presidents, travel the world, carry the Book to hundreds of places—prestigious and remote, praising and extolling the Mighty One, and telling of the saving blood of the Lamb." —US Navy Medicine, Apr 1971, page 8.

"No injury created by the mischance of war is more devastating to youth than the amputation of a limb. The deformity is obvious, the loss permanent, the disability lifelong...The therapeutic objective has been to provide a satisfactory milieu* in which the new amputee can gain a realistic view of his injury and actively begin to reconstruct his life at the outset...The distortion of body image is one of the major concerns of the new amputee." —Rehabilitation of the Acute War Amputee, LT

D. Seligson, MC, USNR, Naval Hospital in USS Sanctuary, DaNang Harbour, RVN, US Navy Medicine, Apr 1971, p. 14. (*milieu—*mil-your*, the atmosphere or setting in which something occurs)

I had never had so many people swirling around me! I'm now in a small room. The Navy procedure aboard USS Sanctuary is as follows: Patient arrives from the field within an hour of injury. Hopefully, there has been a minimum of shock, sepsis**, pain or fear. The patient is then met in Triage by surgeons, chaplains, and hospital corpsmen. His vitals are stabilized, necessary X-rays are taken, and pre-opt is completed. The injured extremities, still covered by battle dressings, shows evidence of dirt, sand, and grass on the hurriedly bandaged wounds. The surgical procedure begins...(**sepsis, a whole body inflammatory state)

There are bright lights over-head. White masked men are women are all around me...yelling...a few cursing. Everything is muffled. *"Where am I? I'm still alive...still alive...still...."*

It would be three weeks before I began returning to full conscious-ness. I was flown to the island of Guam to continue my recovery. Fever became my constant friend. Higher fever. Doctors continuously talking around me. *"What are they writing? What are they saying?"* They always spoke just out of range of my hearing. They emptied many IV bottles into my veins. There was always the sharp wet smell of surgical alcohol. More surgeries...13 of them.... over and over and over again. *"Mom and Dad!"* Their faces began coming powerfully into my mind. *"I want to see Mom and Dad*!" I wanted to feel their arms around me. I wanted to be held by them and I wanted to hold them in my arms. These two vastly important people—were now, the most important human beings in my life. They were the ones I had hurt the deepest, the ones I had abused and tormented. How could I have done all that? They were the ones who loved me unconditionally, with or without legs. *"My body! What happened? No boots. No feet. No legs... Where did the jungle go? Where are my men? This isn't real...this isn't real...no, no, it isn't real, how could it be?"* *"Tim! Tim! Can you hear me?"* said the nurse. *"Sergeant, can you open your eyes?"* *"Tim!"*

Endless bodies, voices, people with bottles, needles, sponges, towels, medicine, swabs, thermometers...*"Tim! Can you look at me?"* And suddenly, one day, everything became clear in my mind. *"I am*

Tim Lee. I am a Marine. I was walking point in Quang Nam Province. The elephant grass. The South Koreans on my right flank. We had just passed an old Buddhist monastery. I'm looking down at the ground. I'm holding my metal detector. The next man is a few meters behind me. I'm walking slowly...I was...walking point...and...and then...and then I was suddenly looking 'up' at everyone around me. Why are they all standing around me? Why is the sky so dark? Why are my ears ringing so violently? What is that smell?

Spent powder, foul smelling black powder was burning my eyes and the inside of my nose. I can taste it on my tongue. *"Have I been hit? Yes, yes, Tim, you got hit. I don't think you have any legs. Look down. Look down. Can you reach down there and see? See for yourself. No, Tim, there's no legs. The bed sheet goes just a few inches below my waist and then it falls limply away, clinging to the mattress. There is almost nothing there. I feel over the rest of my remaining body. Everything else is there...just not the legs and the feet. Okay...okay...I got hit and my legs are gone. Okay, we'll live with this. We'll make it, son. You can do this. You can do this, Tim."*

No one today with the exception of my wife Connie, my sweet mother and siblings in McLeansboro, and of course my beloved father, John Lee, my ultimate hero who has gone on to be with Jesus, and a few close friends know the above described Tim Lee. They remember him all too well. He, today, is known as "boss" as "Dad" as "husband" as "close friend" as "evangelist" and as "Marine", but by the grace of our Lord, he is a totally changed new man, a *new creature* as Paul says. The term "creature" in 2 Corinthians 5.17, is *Ktisis* in the Greek, a newly founded one, a newly established individual, after the rabbinical usage—a man converted from idolatry, literally, the total sum of a newly created being—one who has risen from the mud and mire of an old life, one who has been transformed by the Gospel.

The word "new", *kainos*, signifies freshly made, unused, unworn, *unprecedented*, novel, uncommon, unheard of! I shout with Job through the ages, "For he maketh sore, and bindeth up: he woundeth, *and his hands make whole.*" (Job 5.18) Tim Lee today is a man totally surrendered to a new power—the power of the God of the Bible. One who is "in Christ Jesus"..."a new creature." (Galatians 6.15)

This Marine was indeed broken—physically, mentally and emotionally. John Keble writes, "The word 'broken' used in Psalm 51.17 ("The sacrifices of God are a broken spirit: a broken and a contrite heart...") translates 'crushed, broken in pieces, torn, and brought to birth!' The word 'contrite' means 'collapsed physically or mentally.'" The dictionary defines the word broken as *"Incomplete; forcibly separated into two or more pieces, violated, humbled, weakened and infirmed."*

In the attempt to re-gather my mind and begin thinking about what had happened to me, I realized that although war had taken my legs, there was a far greater power at work in my life on 8 March, 1971 than mere war. Frederick Buechner has said it beautifully in *Whistling in the Dark*, "Whenever you find tears in your eyes, especially unexpected tears, it is well to pay the closest attention. They are not only telling the secret of who you are, but more often than not of the mystery of where you have come from and are summoning you to where you should go next."

Psalm 147:10 says, "He delighteth not in the strength of the horse: he taketh not pleasure in the legs of a man." God had not been impressed with my athletic abilities, my intense running (both physically and mentally) from Him. I had been the arrogant Asahel of 2 Samuel 2.19, pursuing the mighty warrior Abner, running gloriously like a wild deer, at full bore in the field, refusing to turn aside from any danger. I had absolutely no fear of ever being injured in Vietnam. It could NOT happen to me. It was only 30 days till my tour was over. I was offered a desk job. I turned it down. I would live forever. Life for me was one big party.

God could wait until I finished my revellings, or, as Augustus Strong defines it "my nocturnal, riotous activity, my parading through the streets in honor of the false deity of pleasure—my drinking parties till late at night and enjoying every indulgence." I drank to the celebration of eternal youth. But now, after March 8 of 1971, I was celebrating the three inches and the eleven inches I had left of my two legs. I was enduring the sharp, electrical shooting phantom pains that set the end of my stubs on fire. And there was the joy of waking up at 2:00 AM in the morning and finding myself attempting to scratch my itching toes that were no longer there.

"Was this a body? Was this any kind of life? What would women think of me?" I had stood an even six foot tall. I could put my elbow over a basketball rim. I could run and shoot with the best athletes in Illinois. I could, like Asahel of old, run like a deer. I had the ribbons and medals and a track scholarship offer and the accolades of, coaches and players. I could have written my own ticket in the sports world. But the Marines, a hellish war, and God Almighty had brought all of that to an end. Broken! Wounded! Half a man! How would I look racing around the square in McLeansboro in the cold steel of a wheelchair? I could avoid the world as many double amputees decided to do. How about the circus? I could hide behind the confines of a cheap apartment room, draw my government pay and live off Uncle Sam. But this was not the character of a Lee.

My father had won a bronze star in the south Pacific during WWII and then had built an impeccable reputation in our town as a highly respected pastor. The Lees were fighters! Overcomers. The words of scripture began flooding my mind.

Proverbs 3:12, **"For whom the LORD loveth he correcteth; even as a father the son in whom he delighteth."** Deuteronomy 8:5 said, *"Thou shalt also consider in thine heart, that, as a man chasteneth his son, so the LORD thy God chasteneth thee."*

Job 5:17 really hit home to my heart, **"Behold, *happy is the man whom God correcteth:* therefore despise not thou the chastening of the Almighty."** The corrected man is to be happy in the Lord his God, and he is not to despise or become angry at the discipline of the One Who loves him most.

After arriving back in the states, I watched men die in my ward at the Philadelphia Naval Hospital with injuries much less serious than mine. I watched them fall into black despair. I watched them quit, give up, withdraw into oblivion. I watched their wives reject them and leave them. It was as if I was imprisoned in a ward of doom. Once, Will Rogers, the famous wit and comedian, was entertaining at the Milton H. Berry Institute in Los Angeles. The facility was a hospital that specialized in the rehabilitation of polio victims and patients with broken bodies and extreme handicaps.

The great Oklahoma cowboy had everyone in stitches, including the doctors and nurses. Some patients almost fell off their beds laughing at his antics. But suddenly, Rogers left the platform he had been performing on. He walked quickly to the men's room. Was he ill? No. Milton Berry, the man who had accompanied him to the institute found him leaned against the wall, weeping like a brokenhearted child for the patients in the Institute! He dried his tears and went right back out and picked up where he left off. There would be no self pity for Tim Lee! This would *not* be my lot! I would *live!* I rejoiced in Ezekiel 37:5, **"Thus saith the Lord GOD unto these bones; Behold, I will cause breath to enter into you, *and ye shall live*.**" Ezekiel said "turn yourselves, and live..." (Ez 18.32) Again in Ezekiel 16.6, He said, "I said unto thee when thou wast in thy blood, *Live;* yea, I said unto thee when thou wast in thy blood, *Live* (!)

Broken, yes, but this was the new body God had given me. This was the new man. This was the new normal; the new life; the new opportunity; the new future! This new body would carry me over 2 million miles in air flights; to over 3,000 churches and public school assemblies, and to remote parts of the world. I would find myself preaching to crowds numbering into the thousands and tens of thousands. Governors, United States Senators and Congressmen, athletes, celebrates and hundreds and hundreds of Marines.

Jamey Ray is a super talented musician and arranger. He is a Professor at the acclaimed Rollins College in Orlando, Florida. Jamey is an accomplished pianist, even though he was born without his left hand. When Jamey was five years old, his mother Susan was dropping him off for his first day in Kindergarten. As she handed Jamey his lunch, she gave him a kiss and very skillfully asked him a question. "Jamey, what are you going to tell the kids about your body?" Jamey's eyes looked directly into his mother's eyes and the little man replied, "Mother, *there's nothing wrong with my body.*" Jamey had the body God gave him and he was proud of it!

George Washington, at the end of the Revolutionary War was addressing a group of angry officers. The men were complaining about their back pay and the loss of benefits after serving their country so valiantly. They were considering an armed reprisal against the Government. Washington, who was not expected to attend the meeting, surprised the men with his appearance. They were not impressed that he decided to attend the meeting. He addressed the men with a speech. There was only silence when he finished. He then began reading a letter from a member of Congress explaining the financial struggles the government was facing.

As Washington was reading the letter, he suddenly pulled out a pair of reading glasses and put them on. Hardly anyone present knew he wore glasses. They were amazed. Washington then said *"Gentlemen, you will permit me to put on my spectacles, for I have not only grown gray but almost blind in the service of my country."* The statement had immediate effect on the men. Their spirits were broken. Some of them quietly sobbed. Washington finished the letter and without further comment left the building. The officers, all of them brave men, voted unanimously to drop their grievances.

We may be broken, but we're not beaten. Broken, but not defeated. Broken, but not used up. Broken to serve, to mend, to bring others to an amazing Saviour. Broken to minister and to heal.

Chapter Eight

"Dealing with Doubt"

DAVID EDWARDS – Oklahoma City, OK
www.DaveTown.com

David Edwards is an "itinerant postmodern pastor". For more than a decade, he has been sharing his unique brand of ministry to a postmodern generation, as he speaks more than 500 times each year to over 250,000 people. David speaks from his heart about issues relevant to the postmodern generation.

Regardless of the setting, David's message is simple: helping people to discover the importance of a Christ-centered lifestyle and reintroduce the truth of God's Word by meeting people where they are in life and bringing them one step closer in the process of knowing and becoming like Jesus Christ. David is beloved across America and an international evangelist and booked annually to minister at some of the largest venues sharing God's Word. He is ideal for any audiences and perfect for singles and students. He has authored 13 books and hails from Oklahoma.

JOHN the Baptist was a man's man. He was into the whole back to nature thing long before it was popular. The man ate locust and dipped them in wild honey...by choice! He wore camel hair next to his skin. He lived and slept in the desert and every time he opened his mouth, some religious leader got verbally slapped. The people loved him.

They came by the hundreds to hear him speak and to see him baptize new believers in the Jordan River. The religious leaders were curious too. They came if for no other reason than to let everyone know this rogue preacher didn't intimidate them. He preached, they cringed, the people cheered, and John became an influence that had to be eliminated.

John's influence grew quickly and his sermons empowered the people's thinking. Many were beginning to challenge the religious status quo. John gave equal time to the political front too. His talks included exposure of king Herod's illicit lifestyle. Not only a religious target but also he carried a political bulls eye on his back as well. The religious leaders would never have done anything directly to silence John. That would be wrong for them to do. But should King Herod, the Roman appointed ruler of Israel hear enough of John's condemnation, he would take action.

John was a man who lived what he believed. He stood up for what he knew to be true, regardless of the price. He was bold and he spoke out freely. Until now, the price he had to pay for his boldness had been ridicule and disfavor among the religious leaders. When Herod had heard enough, he increased **John's personal cost, he had him arrested.**

John sat in his cell unable to do what he loved. He missed the river; he missed the sun and the fresh air. He longed for the sound of the wind blowing through the trees. He missed the people's hungry ears. He missed connecting with them through his words. He missed the water of the Jordan. He was allowed visitors and some of his closest disciples came to visit him. They encouraged him as best they could with some fresh locust, a small pot of honey and some news about a new preacher who had appeared on the scene. John had met this man a few months back.

That day was particularly memorable for John. The crowds of people were there, he preached his favorite sermon on repentance and at invitation time, this man came forward for baptism. There was something quite different about this man. More than the way he walked or carried himself. There was a quiet confidence oozing from every part of him. Something communicated that the important things in this man's life were settled and not up for debate.

Whether the people recognized it, John did. For the first time, he wondered if this man could be the one that he would introduce. John knew that his ministry would immediately foreshadow the Messiah. Could this man be the long awaited Messiah? He dared not ask the question outright. Still, there was no denying there was something special about this man. If only he had a window to look out of. If a small breeze could just find it's way onto his face. If he could just look at the sky, he would gladly shade his eyes from the blinding sun. All he had were his memories and the news from his disciples.

He listened as they told him of the many miracles and teachings of this man. "Could he be the one?" they asked John. If so what was to become of John and his ministry? What was to become of the people who followed John and his teaching? His disciples had a look of panic and concern on their faces. He stopped their questions with a small hand gesture.

"I am the voice calling in the wilderness, I am the one sent to preach and prepare the way for the Lord. I have done what I was called to do. Whether I preach again or remain here until I die, you must follow him. He must increase...I must decrease." They knew exactly what John was saying without saying it. They knew this would be the last time they would be together. They stood, embraced their leader and left him to face his short-term future as he had lived his life...alone.

The guard closed the door to his cell and John heard the chains lock it closed. No light entered the room; this cell was the reserved for those awaiting execution. Though his eyes had not adjusted to the darkness John made his way to the door. He lowered himself to sit on the stone floor near the door. Leaning his forehead on the wood he waited the last few moments until his eyes adjusted so he could see the slender shafts of light that came through the cracks in the door. Then he waited.

Have you ever felt like John the Baptist, full of questions and doubts? Trying to see the light through the cracks of a dark prison door? Have you ever been tempted to abandon character? There is a sign that hangs over our heads. This sign is lighted only at certain times. When it's illuminated it says "Goober". The sign lights up when we feel awkward, embarrassed, and self-consciousness.

When I was in Junior High this sign flashed on and off so frequently it looked like a strobe light. One time in High School I bought a milk shake put it on top of my car while to get in and left it there while I pulled out of the parking lot. Everybody in the restaurant was pointing. I waved back, "Yeah, I know I have a cool car. Thanks!" I drove on. As I pulled up to a stop at an intersection the shake spilled all over the windshield. That sign popped up over my head and flashed off and on. Everybody at the light pointed and laughed. Thinking quickly I rolled down my window and yelled, "Hey did anybody else see the size of that bird?"

Not long ago I spoke at a University Bible Study. There were about 300 students that filled a tiny, old gymnasium. The band led worship and as each song flowed into the next they became more intense and intimate. I was standing in the back of the room. The band played the last song then I was up to speak. As I moved from the back toward the stage my foot caught on the power cord for the lights. I yanked it out of the wall. The room went totally black which made it easier for everyone to see my sign.

We all have goober moments. There will be a time when you'll be out to dinner with some friends. You will all be sitting in the booth enjoying yourselves. You move in the vinyl seat and it makes that sound—you know the one where everyone looks at you and snickers. You spend the rest of the evening trying to re-create that sound just to prove that sound didn't come out of you. When the Goober moments come, laugh, I promise you'll live through them.

There will be times when you have doubt. There are certain situations that all of us will go through which are going to cause us to doubt: The business person experiences the death of a dream, the teenager with the loss of a friend, the husband with the loss of a job, couples facing a broken marriage. Adults facing mid-life crisis asking, "What am I doing?" The mom with the prodigal child wonders, "Is this Christian life thing really true?" The disillusioned believer asks, "Have I just been good for no apparent reason?" The failed magician ponders, "Has this all just been a hoax?" There have been times in my own life that make me wonder if there really is a God. When the unthinkable appears, trust turns to doubt and our sense of direction, protection, and confidence is shaken.

Doubt is not the lack of trust. The essence of doubt is being caught between two different beliefs at the same time. I've done a lot of ski retreats and the slopes are absolutely beautiful from my hotel window. My windows are always right outside the beginner slope so I get to watch everyone learn how to ski. Almost to a person the beginning skier starts down the slope with their skis taking on a life of their own. They each head off in different directions until the person is split so far that they fall backwards with their skis in the air. That's the way doubt makes us feel. We feel completely caught between two beliefs and unable to do anything to stop the progress so we just fall down. This is exactly what is happening to John. His heart is divided. He knew that his ministry was to precede the ministry of the Messiah. But it appears that his life will soon taken. Did he run his course? Was his life what it should have been? Or did he miss the mark?

And it came about that when Jesus had finished giving instructions to his twelve disciples, he departed from there to teach and preach in their cities. Now when John in prison heard the works of Christ, he sent word by his disciples and he said to him, "Are you the coming one or should we look for someone else?" Matthew 11:3

John was asking, "Jesus, have I lived my whole life for a myth? Have I laid my life on the line for something that is not true? Are you really the one? Should we look for someone else?" Darkness had positioned itself close enough to John to de-create all God had done in and through his ministry. What the enemy wanted most was to choke the faith out of John. John was locked in his struggle to stay lit.

Feel Your Theology

Good theology is what pulls you through a time of doubt. John had to reach deep into all that he had believed and preached in order to silence the rising panic. What he had proven to be true through the living of his life, he now held onto with all his mental might. Even this was challenged by his circumstances. Theology alone is not enough. In order for us to find the strength to face the challenge, we must own theology at the deepest parts of our life. It is like eating a meal prepared by a gourmet chef: the food must be tasted, eaten, and digested before it becomes part of our bodies. Our emotions must submit to theology. If they don't our emotions will run out of control and lead us to into uncertainty, guilt, and fantasy.

Jesus' response to John is strategic. He didn't say, "John, stay right there I'm going to come and put my arm around you, it's going to be okay." He didn't have the Florida boys come to his cell and break into a big southern gospel concert featuring "I'll Fly Away." He didn't send a little greeting card with a scripture on the bottom of it. Do you know what Jesus did? He told John's disciples, "You send Him my word." And Jesus answered and said to them, "Go and report to John the things which you hear and see. "The blind receive sight, the lame walk, the lepers are cleansed, the deaf hear, the dead are raised up, and the poor had the gospel preached to them and blessed is he who keeps from stumbling over me." Matthew 11:4-5

Reading this might not make much sense at first, but the message Jesus sent to John was in New Testament code. When John heard these words he knew exactly what they meant. Let me give you a modern paraphrase of this verse. Imagine that you are facing a moment of intense doubt and Jesus was to send you a letter containing these words. It would read:

John, I am the Christ, in control and committed. Love, Jesus

Imagine John sitting in his cell and the card above was slid under his cell door. When he read what Jesus had written him, this is what he heard. 1) I am the Christ; 2) I am in control; 3) I am committed. These three things are important to us because they reassure us of Christ's character. Our assurance in the midst of doubt depends on our grasp of his character.

Jesus made himself the issue. When doubt arrives in our lives the issue is never the circumstances we face it is our grasp of his character in our lives. In times of doubt, we are faced with two options: to forfeit everything we have lived for or to go back to the foundation of our faith—the character of God himself.

Oz Guinness in his book God in the Dark calls this the "Square One Principle". He explains, "If we give up then we abandon faith all together. But if we go back to Square One we will find a faith that is solid and secure. The lesson of the Square One Principle is this: the person who has the courage to go back when necessary is the one who goes on in the end." We must go back to the basics before going forward

He is the Christ.

Jesus reminded John who he was. I know it feels differently than this, but doubt is primarily about who our trust is in. John sat alone in that dungeon with all the props of his life knocked out from under him. Even though the letter is quite brief, Jesus identified himself as the Messiah.

In verse 5 Jesus was quoting Isaiah 61:1, "The spirit of the Lord is upon me, because he has anointed me to bring good news to the afflicted. He has sent me to bind up the broken hearted, to proclaim liberty to the captives." This Old Testament passage is a Messianic verse. John knew that whoever was able to perform these acts was indeed the Messiah. As John read these words from his cell, I'm sure the message he heard was, "My dear brother, I am the Christ. You have put your faith in the right guy."

Jesus is legit...he is the real deal. He is the Messiah. He fulfilled every one of the prophecies about the Messiah. We need to let the legitimacy of Jesus penetrate our lives. When it does it puts a "no-stick" surface on our souls. Doubt has a much harder time finding a place to stick. When this truth penetrates our lives, we will find the beginnings of a trust that will allow us to live authentically in the midst of doubt. A trust that stands in the face of doubt is a faith grounded in the truth of who Christ is.

He is in Control.

"Go and report to John the things which you have hear and see..." Matthew 10:4 Jesus reminds John that he is in control of circumstances. Regardless of how things appear, he is still the ruler. In verse 4 Jesus is speaking of his present demonstration of power. John's disciples had followed Jesus for several days just to observe his ministry. They had seen many miracles and had heard him speak. They had seen him rule and reign over all kinds of sickness and pain. Christ's ministry was powerfully at work.

The focus of Jesus' ministry was to make the kingdom of God visible. He overcame the darkness by healing the wounded. When John's eyes fell upon these words he heard Jesus say, "John, the kingdom is

advancing. All is going as planned. You have done your part, you introduced me well."

He is Committed

"And blessed is he who keeps from stumbling over me." Matthew
11:6

To put this verse another way, "do not be offended by the Lord". It
would have been easy for John to stumble over Jesus. Doubt is hard and
lonely and John felt it intensely. He was still a young man. Not old and
useless. Yet, he had lived as he was told to live, spoke what he was told
to speak. And the apparent reward was to be relieved of his head. All the
while Jesus walked freely about the land.

Doubt and unbelief are not the same things. At this point, John is
not in a state of unbelief; he is not willfully refusing to believe. Rather
his expectations are colliding with his doubt. If his doubt is not properly
confronted, it could grow into unbelief. The same is true for any of us.
When some of our expectations about God are not met, it's easy to take
offense and to say, "Why didn't God do...." Or "Why would God allow
that to happen?" Or, "If this is the way God treats his people..."

It would be easy to believe that God is mad, angry, unfair, disgusted,
uninterested, and indifferent towards us. In reality, God is understanding, aware, present, involved, working, and committed. Theology
and feelings are connected. In a season of doubt we must let what we
know invade what we feel. When John read this line of the letter he
could hear Jesus saying, "John, even though the dungeon of doubt is
dark and you will suffer, but I am committed to you."

Believe it or not, I can hear your thoughts. You are saying, "Right!
That sounds good. That sounds very sweet and devotional but is it real?
And does it work?" I want to tell you how these three words brought me
though a major time of doubt.

I had met this girl and I totally fell for her. Her name was Nezi. She
was a "G3"—godly, gorgeous, and great. A believer who had led each
one of her family members to Christ, she was a sharp, very articulate
lawyer with her own law practice in downtown Rio. (I had to go to
South America to get a date, but that's a whole other story.) She was

my interpreter for an eight-day revival at First Baptist Church in Rio. I spoke in all the schools in the area, and I taught Bible studies in the towns from house to house. And everywhere I went; she went—which was kind of like having a first date that went on for over a week. Very cool!

I returned to Brazil about six months later, and she was my interpreter once again. The more time I spent with her, the more respect I had for her and the more I was drawn to her. We spoke at a school where I told the students who Jesus is and what he has done. I talked about how awesome He is and if you give your life to Him, your life will be different forever. I gave an invitation and 110 students stood up. I thought that couldn't be right, they must have thought I said, who wants free pizza.

So I had them all sit down and I started all over again. Again, I got to the point where I gave the invitation and I said to Nezi, "You don't need me, you just give it." She stood up and I sat down. She started giving the invitation in Portuguese and 110 students stood up again. It was amazing!

A woman who knows the things of God and how to communicate them, Wow! That is very attractive to me. Besides that, she could speak English, but not enough to argue...perfect. No stress, no fighting and low maintenance.

On my third trip to Brazil, I made sure I had about four days off—just to be with Nezi. She drove me all around Rio and took me to eat at this little restaurant that jutted out into the Atlantic Ocean. If you've never been to Rio or seen pictures of the city, you know that in the middle of the city is that big Christ statue.

It is 120 feet tall sitting on a mountain that's 2,000 feet high. Christ has his arms out and they are 48 feet across. We walked up the 220 steps to the base of the statue. The mid-afternoon sun cast a shadow of Christ across us. That was the first place I ever kissed her. There couldn't be a better Christian date. To kiss her in the shadow of Jesus and his outstretched arms. That was the coolest date of my life.

I left there telling her, "I'm going to bring you to America in December. I do a lot of conferences and I want you to see the ministry and what I do in America."

I kept in touch by phone—at a dollar a minute—anticipating our time together. One day as I had finished packing and had my bags in my hands to head to the air port, I got a call from one of my missionary friends in Brazil. He said Dave, "I'm calling about Nezi." I said, "Yeah, she great isn't she?" He said, "No, you don't understand. Yesterday in downtown traffic, someone reached into her car window and cut her throat." I never saw her again.

I had to pack my bags, stand up in those youth conferences, and talk about how great Jesus is. I won't lie to you; it was the darkest time of my life. I told God, "I work for you. You are all-powerful and all knowing. You know what the deal is. You could have protected or stopped that from happening."

It was these 3 things that pulled me through that time of doubt. I was long passed needing some emotional experience, or some new song. I didn't need someone hugging me telling me, "It's going to be okay." I had to get up everyday that month and speak twenty-seven times knowing that she was supposed to be with me. I had to boldly proclaim the gospel while I was fighting doubt in my own personal life.

It was very difficult for me not to just walk away from everything. The only way I got through it was to sit down and begin and end my day moving through these 3 things. I put my trust in the right person. He is who he says he is. I've not lived my life for a myth. Just because it cost me someone I loved dearly, does not make it all a myth.

I know Jesus is real because he is the Christ. He is in control, and he is committed. He is who he says he is. I believe it. I let that truth sink deep within my life. I understand that his power is awesome. I understand that it may cost me and test me to my last thread. I may not be able to take it, but it is still true.

At those times when we feel powerless, we must remember that God hears the powerless. Their prayers are answered. At the deepest moment of doubt and at our weakest moments, that is where the presence of God is. The powerless are always heard and the suspicious are answered. Jesus came for people who are in situations where doubt and suspicions are combined with fear and panic. We must live our lives in such a way that they can see his character in us and through us. The world of darkness longs to see if this Christ really is who he says he is. They long to see a life that proves he is who we say he is. They ache to watch character in action.

I don't know what your situation is. I don't know what has happened to make you feel like a goober. I don't know your pain, I only know mine. But hopefully through the sharing of my victory over doubt you can find the confidence that Christ is who he says he is. Hopefully you will find the strength to persevere.

Perseverance is possible. Because of these events in my life, I am able to stand in front of students and tell them the truth. Perseverance is possible. You can go on. There are still times in my life when the weather is right or I hear a certain song I think of **Nazi**. I could be in a place that reminds me of where I used to sit and talk with her. All the emotions are set off again, but what pulls me through those dark times is the light of Christ. John the Baptist must have felt it in the dark cell, just before he was beheaded. I have seen that light in my darkest times. If you look, just look, you'll see it too!

Throughout the centuries many have attempted to extinguish the light of Christ. But there has always been a witness to the character and life of Christ. The darkness has never and never will be able to overcome the light of the life found in Jesus Christ. "From the time of John the Baptist until now the kingdom of heaven suffers violence, and violent men take it by force."

Matthew 11:12 The battle John faced in the darkness of his prison cell while he awaited death is the same battle Jesus faced on the cross while dying. It is also the same battle you and I face daily as we seek to flesh out the life of Christ in a world that seeks to overcome us. The kingdom of heaven has always suffered attacks but it has always prevailed.

Victory for the God's kingdom of light is assured when you and I take our place in the battle of light over darkness. To the extent we embrace the character of Christ we determine the success of the light in this world. You are the light of the world! Get LIT. Stay LIT. Love LIT.

Chapter Nine

"King of Ring meets King of all Kings"

LEX LUGER – A<small>TLANTA</small>, *GA*
www.FlexwithLex.org

Lawrence Wendell "Larry" Pfohl (born June 2, 1958), better known by his ring name Lex Luger, is an American former professional wrestler and football player currently working with WWE on their wellness policy. He is best known for his work with the National Wrestling Alliance (NWA), World Championship Wrestling (WCW), and the World Wrestling Federation (WWF).

Among other accolades in professional wrestling, Luger is a three-time World Champion, having held the WCW World Heavyweight Championship twice and the WWA World Heavyweight Championship once; a record-tying five-time NWA/WCW United States Heavyweight Champion, and the longest-reigning champion in history; and the 1994 WWF Royal Rumble winner (with Bret Hart). Readers of *Pro Wrestling Illustrated* voted Luger the Most Popular Wrestler of the Year 1993.

Today, Lex is a child of God and speaks to hundreds of thousands of people annually in schools, prisons, crusades and church revivals. He is still a man with a mission but more than ever a man with a message. He serves on Advisory Board of Praisefest Ministries "Cruise with a Cause" and together they have witnessed nearly 40,000 come to faith in Christ. Lex and former World Wrestling Champion Nikita Koloff "The Russian Nightmare" also speak and teach both the Gospel & Wellness seminars for others to become "The Total Package" in Christ www.FlexWithLex.Org

Lex is a dear friend of Frank Shelton and this chapter was written and used by permission from both Luger and Dr Harris, editor of GA Baptist Press.

\\

"THE Total Package" and "The Narcissist" — gained worldwide fame as a pro wrestling champion. He stood at 6-feet 4-inches tall, weighed 265 pounds and had a 32-inch waist. His muscles were like polished steel and his perfectly sculptured body added to the wrestling mania that had gripped the nation. He frequently highlighted his muscular physique by posing in front of full-length mirrors before many of his matches. His wrestling persona was designed to thrill his fans. His accomplishments in the ring are legendary.

For the last five and a half years, he's also been a Christian, learning and growing more each day. God, he says, has helped him "get rid of the last remnant of that vanity and pride" that was the emblem of his ring persona. Born in 1958, Luger played professional football in the Canadian Football League and the now-defunct United States Football League before beginning his wrestling career. Lex was blessed to have two loving parents who are loving, caring people but he didn't begin to attend church much later as an adult. He never went to church early on but grew up chasing fame in the WCW and WWE on a track that included drugs, alcohol and women.

"My life was a train wreck," Luger admitted. "I was burning the candle at both ends. I had a beautiful wife, Peggy, and two wonderful children, Brian and Lauren. But I was living one life on the road and another life at home. I didn't feel like I was accountable to anyone. "I was making millions of dollars and had a lot of fancy stuff — cars, clothes, baubles — and never realized why I wasn't satisfied. I chased a life of folly, a course of trivial pursuit. I had a feeling of invincibility. They called me 'The Cyborg.'

"I had a home with my wife and children on the ninth green of the

Sugarloaf Country Club in Duluth, GA and a townhouse with my girl-friend in Marietta. I thought I was managing and juggling the situation, but I wasn't. Sometimes when you think you've got a grip on life, you really don't. The people I thought were friends were users and abusers. "In 2003 my girlfriend, Elizabeth, died in my arms of an overdose of drugs. I was arrested later that day after a search of the townhouse revealed a number of illicit controlled substances."

The next day Luger was released on $27,500 bail. Elizabeth's death was ruled accidental. Luger pleaded guilty to the drug charges and was given a $1,000 fine, sentenced to five years probation, and required to submit to periodic drug testing. Luger confessed, "I violated probation on numerous occasions. I was caught for reckless driving, continued to drink alcohol and abuse drugs, but somehow God protected me even though I ignored Him. "From May until August of 2005 things went from bad to worse. I could have overdosed at any time. It is a miracle of God that I survived during that period of time."

That August he had a nightmare in his hotel room. He recalled of the dream, "I ended up in the bottom of a pond, asking myself, 'Is this all there is?' I was on drugs at the time and actually think I died and slipped into eternity for a few moments. Suddenly, I sat up, looked up and saw a little spark — a little white light. I was enveloped in darkness, in hell, but sensed that God loved me enough to give me that speck of light.

"When I awoke, I reached for the Bible in that room, but it opened to the genealogies in the book of Genesis. When I saw all those unfa-miliar names, I concluded that the answer was not in the Bible and threw it against the wall. Although I didn't understand what was happening, that was the moment of a spiritual awakening for me."

In the latter part of that year Luger decided to make a comeback in Winnipeg, Manitoba. However, he and two fellow wrestlers were removed from a flight from Minneapolis to Winnipeg and he was held without bond due to his outstanding felony charges and failing to obtain permission to leave the country from his parole officer. After remaining in the Hennepin County (Minn.) jail for two weeks, he was extradited to Georgia to stand trial.

Lex was sentenced to three months in the Cobb County jail where he began to receive visits from Steve Baskin, a Baptist pastor in Kennesaw. When he was told that a pastor had come to visit him, Luger shouted, "I don't want to talk to any preacher!" During this time of incarceration, Baskin was continuously visiting others in the jail. Luger would persistently wave him away, indicating that he had no interest in talking.

Then Baskin started smuggling small containers of peanut butter to Luger, who claimed he was always hungry. Lugar also knew that the only way to get out of the "pod" was to see the pastor/chaplain. He started accepting Baskin's visits, and a relationship ensued. By March of 2006 Luger was released from the jail and went back to the same extended stay hotel room where he had overdosed and had had the nightmare the previous August.

One day he happened to meet Baskin at Gold's Gym and the preacher asked "The Total Package" to help him get into shape, to become his physical trainer. Lex said he thought to himself, "I will give him a workout he will never forget. I am going to make him so sore, he'll never set foot in a gym again." Luger's idea of an impossible workout schedule for Baskin didn't work. Baskin kept coming back for more. The wrestler admitted, "I couldn't run him off."

The people in the gym began to ask Luger who he was training and when he replied, "He's a preacher, a jail chaplain," they were in shock. Luger remarked, "Steve started taking me to all kinds of places — to places like Golden Corral and Wal-Mart. I would never have been caught dead in Wal-Mart, but I soon realized he was taking me to places where my fans were. I was shocked at people's reactions.

"He also started giving me books to read like Josh McDowell's 'Answers to Tough Questions.' He would leave Gospel tracts in his car, and when he would go into a store I would read those tracts. "Then on April 16, 2006, he talked me into going to church on a Sunday night. I went to Clarkdale First Baptist Church and heard Pastor Marvin 'Doc' Frady preach on Matthew 7:24-29. He told about a man who built his house on the sand and another man who built his house on a rock. "I felt like God was speaking through him to me. I could see all my stuff on sand with no foundation. All my life was built on shifting sand and was nothing more than a house of cards. My empire was not built on a rock, but sand.

"I went back to my room — the same room where I had that nightmare — and Doc's message was churning in my heart. Steve came and explained God's plan of salvation. It was hard for me to understand how God could forgive me for all the sins in my life, because I had made such a mess of things. "Steve told me that God wanted to give me eternal life and a home in heaven where I could live with Him eternally. He told me that I would receive the gift of the Holy Spirit. I got on my knees and prayed and asked God to forgive me and save me.

"When I got up I was crying, and that light, which I had seen as a speck of light six months earlier, became a surge of light purging the darkness out of my body. I did not understand it all then, but it was so powerful I didn't think my earthly vessel could contain it.

"I never felt stronger. I felt a power inside of me that I interpreted as the power of the Holy Spirit. "Even after my spinal injury I was not defeated. I could say with Paul, 'Most gladly therefore will I glory in my infirmities, that the power of Christ may rest upon me.'" "Doc" Frady has become Luger's mentor and spiritual father. They meet regularly to study the Bible and pray.

Frady said, "After his salvation I saw Lex pour six $6,000 bottles of wine down the drain. I have watched him grow in the Lord, memorize the Word of God and boldly share his faith. "People told me that he would be back in jail in six months, but it has been more than five years and he is as solid as a rock. I wouldn't be afraid to have him speak anywhere as a representative of Christ." Luger said God used a 2007 episode to rid him of his vanity. In October of that year he had just completed a strenuous workout and boarded a plane in Atlanta for San Francisco. During the flight he was talking with the person next to him and experienced a sudden nerve impingement in his neck. With the temporary paralysis he was unable to turn his head and remained facing his seatmate for the next three hours.

After landing, Luger went to his hotel and laid down to rest. When he awoke he was suffering from a searing, hot, stabbing pain that was almost unbearable.

"It was a perfect storm," Luger explained. "The workout had

inflamed the muscles in my neck and shoulders. I was also dealing with arthritis and bone spurs. I had held my neck in a fixed position on the plane for three hours. "All that combined to cut off the flow of blood to my central cord and resulted in what I thought was going to be a temporary paralysis."

A month after the "spinal stroke" Luger was still in a quadriplegic state, having no movement in his arms or legs. He had surrendered to Christ but "was still trying to be a super muscular poster boy. I was trying to be 27 at age 47, but God had to get rid of my vanity," Luger said. "I had trouble letting go of the old Lex physically. My human fleshly nature didn't want to let go of what had come to be billed as 'The Total Package.' I guess God had to help me get rid of the last remnant of that vanity and pride."

Although Luger's neurological episode paralyzed him for months and robbed him of 70 pounds of muscle, he is stronger than ever. "The Total Package" has been unwrapped and rewrapped by the transforming power of Christ. "It's been an incredible five-and-a-half years," Luger said "but I have learned that God is with us through whatever challenges we face."

Chapter Ten

"Well Done, Thy Good & Faithful Servant"

PASTOR CHRISTIAN HARRIS – WALDORF, MD
www.ThePointeMinistries.org

Rev. Christian Harris was born on May 11, 1981 in Atlanta Georgia. He began his ministry by singing solos in the church and in the kid's choir later becoming a children's pastor and youth pastor. Today, he serves as senior pastor of The Pointe Ministries in Waldorf Maryland. Pastor Harris desires to thank the loving people at The Pointe who stuck by him and his mom after his father's tragic passing. They are reminded daily of the work that his father started and more importantly, the mission the Lord has set before them.

Pastor Christian dedicates this book to his Mother, Joan Harris, who is the strongest person he's ever known, through everything her faith never waivered but grown! Christian is also the lead singer of a band that is dedicated to Pastor Ron Harris. The name of the band is "4:47" which is the time that Pastor Harris passed away on August 23, 2010. Christian would love to hear from you, to contact him write to pkcobra@aol.com. You can also visit their church website www.thepointeministries.org and the band website at www.rockwith447.com.

HAVE you ever wondered what a true Christian looks like? Or what being a Christian is all about? I have a story that has changed my life forever, and I want to share it with you and I hope it changes your life too!

I was raised in church and have gone to Sunday school and Bible study my whole life. All the churches I have been a member of, my Father was the senior Pastor. My Dad's name was Ronald Wayne Harris and he was a man with a heart after the things of God! He raised his two boys to follow in God's ways and to have a life devoted to the Lord and never part from that path. My Mother is an awesome woman of God who loves the Lord and her family with all of her heart and soul. I am very privileged to have such wonderful parents who show me true love by taking me to church and teaching me the things of God. I strongly believe that if you love someone then you will share the love of God with them, and my parents did just that!

As I mentioned before I have a brother whose name is Ron Harris Jr. and he was raised in the same home as me but chose a different path. Ron was raised in church as well but when he was fourteen or so, he found the wrong crowd and unfortunately, he found the wrong crowd at church. Ron joined and was actively involved in a church youth group in Alabama that was very large. As time went by Ron started developing some very bad habits, he would come home late at night, come home disoriented and his behavior was all over the place. I was very young at the time, but I noticed that something was not right. Ron went down a path where he was addicted to addictions! Ron had to have something as a crutch in his life.

Our family has lived in Georgia, Alabama, Virginia, Florida and Maryland. When we moved to Waldorf Maryland, we pastored a church where Ron came on special occasions but was encouraged to attend on a daily basis. I remember Ron always saying that people were fake in church, and it is sad but I have found that there are many fake people in church, but we must stay focused on God, not people and this is what Ron was told repeatedly by Mom and Dad.

While we were in Maryland Ron started taking a medication called "Adderall" which is a medication used to treat attention deficit disorder. This medication is a mind-altering drug that acts as speed, especially when abused. Ron began to take this medication in mass consumption and would mix it with alcohol. Ron became a different person that would talk to himself, became paranoid, and his trouble with the law became a regular occasion. Our family moved to Davenport Florida in 2008 to pastor a church there. Ron made the move with the rest of the family and at first, everything seemed to be ok with Ron, but as time progressed, things got worse. Ron found a doctor in Florida who refilled the prescription for Adderall and the problems began all over again, but this time they were worse than before. While our family was facing all the problems that Ron was going through, the devil was facing us on yet another front, he was attacking us from every angle. Lies were being spread about my Father that pushed people away from the church we left in Maryland and the people there began to reach out to us in hopes we would come back to Maryland and start a new ministry. I made a decision to go back to Maryland to talk with the people who voiced their concern and want us to come start a new ministry. My Mother and I met with many of the people who sent us messages and we knew it was the Lord's will for us to come back to Maryland and start "The Pointe Ministries!" My Father once told the congregation "church people can be the meanest, nastiest, and most judgmental people in life." We were soon to find this out once again first hand!

One day we received a call from Ron Jr. down in Florida, he was in trouble with the law once again. He was on abusing drugs and alcohol and ran from the police. Once the police finally apprehended Ron Jr., they arrested him and charged him with many fleeing police, reckless driving etc... Ron Jr. was facing a hearing to set the date of his trial and Ron Jr. was very anxious and nervous. My Father decided to take a trip down to Florida after church on Sunday, August 15, 2010 to help Ron in his court date as Mom and I stayed back in Maryland. The week went by and Dad called every day and spoke with Mom on the phone for hours about Ron Jr.'s situation. I overheard many conversations they had, and Dad would say that he's never seen Ron act like this before! Mom would get off the phone and act like nothing was wrong but I knew better than that. I did not ask any questions but I could tell something was definitely wrong and Mom did not want to worry me about it.

At four in the afternoon on Sunday, August 22, we received a call from Dad. He talked to Mom for about an hour, when the call was over Mom came to see me and told me how interesting the phone call was that she had just received from Dad. She proceeded to tell me that they talked about Ron's strange behavior. Dad told her that he had never seen Ron Jr. like this. After an hour, they were getting ready to hang up, Dad said to Mom, "Joan!" then silence, "I love you!" Mom told me that it was strange; it was as if Dad knew something was going to happen to him and he wanted Mom to know he loves her! I know that Mom will never forget that conversation, which was the last time they ever spoke.

Late Sunday night around seven o'clock, we got a call from the sheriff's department down in Florida. I answered the phone and told the officer who I was and the officer told me I needed to call Orlando Regional Hospital as soon as I could because there had been an accident. Mom took the phone, went into a different room and made the call to the Hospital. A few minutes passed when I heard Mom cry out, "Oh no!" A few minutes passed and she came out of the room crying uncontrollably saying that Dad was burned over 60 percent of his body! Mom and I immediately left the house and headed for the Baltimore Airport. We stayed overnight at the airport to catch the earliest flight to Orlando Florida. When we arrived at the Hospital in Florida, they informed us that Dad was under the name "John Doe" to keep his identity hidden from reporters. They placed us into a private room with the doctor who was taking care of Dad and the head nurse. We all sat in this tiny room and the doctor told us what happened.

As we sat in the room on Monday, August 23, we received the worst news that we could have ever received. The doctor looked both of us in the eye and said that Dad chances of living were slim to none. Those were the hardest words I have ever had to listen to! Mom and I cried uncontrollably as all the thoughts ran through our head that Dad will no longer be in our lives. On Monday, August 23, Mom and I went in to see my Father one last time and to say goodbye to him. We went into his room and talked to him, told him we love him and that we were sorry he had to go through this. On August 23, 2010 at 4:47pm, I lost my best friend and my Father!

So what happened? How did this happen? Why was my Father lying in the hospital unconscious and unrecognizable? On Sunday, August 22,

Ron Jr. and my Father got into a disagreement about probably something silly. Ron Jr. was high on the medication and not himself. Dad got up to use the restroom and as he was in the restroom, Ron Jr. went into the garage and mixed gasoline with bleach, went back into the house and threw the mixture into my Father's face then set him on fire. Dad stumbled out the door and into the front yard where neighbors saw him and came to his aid. One of the neighbors was named David who sat with Dad after the fire was put out and he stayed by Dad's side until the ambulance arrived. David asked Dad "Is there was anything I can do?" Dad said, "I want to pray!" Dad's lungs were severely damaged but it was not going to stop him from praying to God Almighty! David and my Father prayed together and when the prayer was over David asked my Father, "Who did this to you?" Dad answered, "My son, and I forgive him!" The helicopter and ambulance arrived and my Father transported by helicopter to Orlando Regional Medical Center in Orlando Florida.

Mom and I were thinking about everything and both of us hoped that someone that knew the Lord would be there to pray with Dad. We strongly believe that brother David was sent by God to be with Dad before he passed away. David told us later that he only was with my Father for ten to fifteen minutes, but that in those few minutes Dad changed his life! That is how my Father was; he genuinely cared for everyone and showed God's love to all he met. My brother walked out of the house after he set my Father on fire and the police could not find him.

The police found my brother the next day behind a store in Florida. My brother was still under the influence of the medication that he was abusing and was clearly not himself. My brother used to preach in his room and love going to church, but one day when he began to abuse drugs and alcohol that all changed. My Mother and Father love my brother one hundred percent and were always there to support him and reach out that helping hand. My brother is currently in a Florida prison where he will probably spend the rest of his life. Mom and I believe that God still has a great work for Ron Jr. in the prison. We believe that Ron Jr. will reconnect with the Lord and let His glory shine in that prison to reach the prisoners that no one else may be able to save! This tragedy affected the community we lived in. The community had a vigil for Dad the following week that was led by the people who helped my Father. People in the community also came up to Mom and me to tell us how Dad had changed their lives. One neighbor told us that Dad was outside walking around the neighborhood praying and the neighbor was going through a very tough situation. The neighbor stopped my Father and told him his situation. The neighbor then told us that Dad stopped at the moment to pray with him in the front lawn. This story is an example of just how much my Father genuinely cared for people. He was truly a man of God, and currently that is hard to find, even among many pastors!

This whole situation has changed my life forever and I know that it has changed more people's lives than I will ever know and I hope this chapter and this book changes your life! Everyone faces battles and struggles in their life, some battles are harder than others are but we all face them. The Bible tells us in the book of Romans chapter five, verses three through five, "Not only so, but we also rejoice in our sufferings, because we know that suffering produces perseverance; perseverance, character; and character, hope. And hope does not disappoint us, because God has poured out his love into our hearts by the Holy Spirit, whom he has given us." God's love conquers all!

When troubles come your way, we should be thankful for these trials because it means we are doing something right! Do not let doubters, nay Sayers, and the devil stop you from doing what the Lord has called you to do! I could have given up, stopped going to church and serving the Lord, but my hope is in the Lord and in His mighty hands! I will never stop serving the Lord, and never lose focus on Him, not man, but on the Lord. People said I was not qualified and not smart enough to lead a congregation but "Greater is He that is within us!" I will not give up, not give in, or water down my faith for anything or anyone. My Father showed me what love was all about during my time on earth with him.

My Mother and Father prayed, "Lord, we want whatever it takes for Ron Jr. to get help and find you again, for that to be done!" Little did they know that Dad would have to die in order for Ron Jr. to get the help he needs. I strongly believe that Ron Jr. is exactly where he needs to be to get free from drugs and have the remainder of his life to get close to God once again. I want to share another Bible verse with you and that is Romans, chapter eight, verse twenty-eight, "And we know that in all things God works for the good of those who love him, who have been called according to his purpose." God has a plan for you, all you have to do is reach out to God, no matter what your past looks like, or what troubles you may be facing, let God be God and know that He is in control.

The church that my Father pastored at the time of his passing was small but filled with people we love and cared for deeply. One of the sermons that my Father preached about a month before his passing was about people leaving the church. Pastor Harris told us that, "People will leave the church, and your jaws will drop at the people who will leave God's will and our church!" After my Father passed, the support from the church was overwhelming but that support from certain people changed to a self-centered state of mind! Leaders in the church walked out on the ministry and our church who said they were behind us and supported us. At that moment in time, all I could think about was Pastor Harris preaching about what I told you earlier, that church people could be the meanest! Well, people left the church and the talk began that our church would not last under my preaching and leadership, but little did they know what the Lord had in store!

My Father was the most amazingly gifted Pastor that I have ever heard (and I have heard plenty of other Pastors).

He had a passion for the Lord and winning the lost to the Lord! I remember Dad would always ask me if I wanted to be a Pastor like him, and I would always tell him that I did not think I could handle that responsibility. After I stood over my Father and watched him take his last breathe on this earth, the Lord told me that it was my time to take the lead and be the Pastor that my Father always knew I would become! I then remembered what the topic of my Father's last sermon was that he preached on August 16 2010. My Father stood in the pulpit of The Pointe Ministries and spoke of "Not being afraid to die!" I know that my Father knew God and had a personal relationship with the Lord. My Father is praising the Lord with all the other saints in heaven and I am very happy for him, but I miss him so very much.

Presently, I am the pastor of The Pointe Ministries in Waldorf, Maryland and I must tell you that the Lord is doing wonderful things at our church. I am honored to be a vessel that the Lord is using to reach people that would never have come to church as usual, but they come because of my Dad's testimony and the Love that is shown through each person. I encourage you to tell everyone about Pastor Harris' story that you have read about in this chapter, and tell them about the love and forgiveness that was shown in the middle of this tragedy.

My Mother, Joan Harris, is the strongest Christian example that I have ever known and I am so blessed, and honored to have such a wonderful Mother! She has not missed a day of church since Dad's passing; she stays strong and is listening to the voice of truth. She not only lost her husband, but her son will be spending the rest of his life in prison. None of that has stopped her from praising the Lord and showing others around her what it really means to be a Christian and to love the Lord. My Mother is starting a ministry for families of people who have family members who struggle with addictions. Mom is no psychiatrist, or doctor, but she is a child of God who wants to let people know that there is someone who cares and wants to talk with him or her, and be there to listen and share. Most importantly, she wants to let everyone know about the greatest friend anyone could ever have and that is Jesus Christ! He will never leave you or forsake you, and when things get tough, He will be there to carry you through.

One of my favorite songs is by Casting Crowns and it is, "Praise You in this storm." I listen to that song all the time because it is so powerful and true. Ask yourself this question, could you give God glory if this happened to you? If this happened to you, would you go to church, lift your hands and make a joyful noise unto the Lord? I know people now who have not gone through anything as tough as this, yet they find an excuse not to go to church to give God the glory. Another song that we sing in church a lot is, "No chains on me" by Chris Tomlin. In the second verse of this song it says, "Abandoned by cold religion, my hearts on fire!" Do not get wrapped up in religion, but get wrapped up in God and His love, let your heart be on fire for the Lord! Life is too short to not live for God and not give Him praise every day. I know that Dad is looking down from heaven with a huge smile on his face, because he loves me and is proud that I am following the call of God in my life! He is proud of my Mother who is staying strong in the Lord and not letting the devil win! I believe that the Lord uses those that are broken, and the most powerful testimonies come from those that have been broken by this world! Without trials and tests, how would we grow? We all have a choice to make, to follow Christ or not. What is your choice?

The last thing I want you to read in this chapter is something my Father always used to say. My Father would say, "Title or testimony!" This meant that he wanted to be known by his testimony and not his title or position. My Dad could not wait to get to heaven and hear the Lord say to him, "*Well done thy good and faithful servant!*" Truly, my Father has heard those words spoken to him by our Master and Savior.

Chapter Eleven

"Hollywood to the Holy Land"

BRANDON CROUCH – SANTA MONICA, CA
www.BrandonCrouch.com

James 1:2 "Blessed is the man who perseveres under trial, because when he has stood the test, he will receive the crown of life that God has promised to those who love him."

Brandon Crouch is an international speaker, host and television personality. He is grandson to Paul and Jan Crouch, founders of the world's largest Christian television studio, TRINITY BROADCAST NETWORK. Their motto: "Coast to coast and around the world" has helped reach multiplied millions for Jesus Christ.

Brandon loves his wife, Marley Crouch more than life itself and they share a home in Santa Monica, CA. He is currently planting a new church in Santa Monica and travels frequently to preach God's Word. Brandon considers it an honor and humbling to see people come to Jesus through the proclamation of the Gospel of Jesus Christ. Brandon's grandmother, Jan Crouch recently built the beautiful Holy Land Experience in Orlando, FL and he has indeed traveled from Hollywood to the Holy Land. Brandon worked in the entertainment industry for over 10 years and loves to utilize the power of media and the gospel together for the glory of Jesus Christ. *"The gospel is the greatest story ever told and I love to effectively tell the story through whatever platform God opens up."* Brandon also takes advantage of social media tools, such as Facebook and Twitter @BrandonCrouch to spread the good news of Jesus Christ.

Along with speaking around the world Brandon often does media seminars that highlight effective ways to use media in your non-profit organization. For more information about Brandon Crouch please visit his website at www.BrandonCrouch.com

---

As eldest grandson to founders of the largest Christian television network in the world, Trinity Broadcasting Network (TBN), my story isn't what most people would imagine it to be. Born on March 7, 1983, my childhood growing up in the epitome of Southern California's suburbia, Irvine, CA. was everything most children dream of.

I was blessed beyond belief to have two wonderful parents who knew the Lord, I lived in beautiful two story home in a safe neighborhood, I naturally excelled in sports, and had more friends than I could count. When it came to matters of the church, however, most would be surprised to find out that I did not grow up on the church pews every Sunday. I come from six generations of Pastors on both sides of my family, and while we lived our lives as Christians, I was certainly not the kid running around the church halls being greeted by strangers that I've only met once in my life.

Instead of growing up in Sunday school memorizing bible verses, singing gospel hymns, and going to church camp, my sisters and I were occupied with sports and friends. My father owned his own production company, PJ Video, a secular company that shot everything from Disneyland commercials to workout infomercials. It was on the set of my father's shoots where I garnered all of my television and media experience, not on grandparent's famous TV network. I saw my grandparents (Paul and Jan Crouch) often but it never really dawned on me as a kid to think what they were doing was touching so many people around the world! They were just grandma and papa to me.

To be brutally honest, I wasn't even fully aware of what TBN really was until I went to college at Oral Roberts University and my classmates began to share with me the profound impact TBN had made in their lives. What I did not know at the time, is that ORU was a breeding ground for the "whose who" of well-esteemed ministers and church leaders kids and grandkids. I quickly found out that carrying the last name of Crouch actually meant something to these people. You can only imagine my shock to be thrown into the political church world that many knew day in and day out of their entire lives!

Before I got to ORU, "Crouch" was just my last name, and "TBN" was my grandparents business, neither one really holding any heavy weight to me; but for the first time in my life, I was surrounded by others that both names were of very serious and prestigious reputation. I was highly criticized for not being spiritual enough, or proper enough. I also had to wear a full suit and tie to school everyday. It was an extreme culture shock to me. After one year, I left ORU to pursue another school a bit closer to home, Point Loma Nazarene University in San Diego, CA. It seemed like a dream come true! What I did not know is that my story of complete brokenness starts here.

Unlike ORU, Point Loma was a mellow atmosphere where no one seemed to care about my name or family association. At first I loved it, but like most 20 year olds, I began to seek after my identity and purpose, and realized that both had very shallow foundations. In attempt to find solace, I quickly turned to girls and partying to fulfill a desire that I could not describe. This lifestyle led to a dark path of brokenness, lone-liness, and self-satisfaction. As a result, spending my time and energy focused on everything but academia, my GPA rapidly declined and within a matter of one year, I got kicked out of school. Embarrassed, rejected, and unsure of where to turn, I moved back home to Orange County and began living paycheck to paycheck with no direction and no real hope for the future.

What I want people to know about being blessed in their brokenness is that this is a fight - not against flesh and blood (well sometimes) but against a dark and evil world. That is why the Bible so many times refers to Satan as "the ruler" of this world. This world represents everything living for the Kingdom is not. The world wants to shame us, beat us, and spit on us while we are down. The world wants to remind us of how pathetic and helpless we are. It's not easy living life on this earth but I can tell you there is hope! When we are living our lives for Jesus, there is nothing that this "big bad world" can take away from us. The Bible calls us to live righteously before Him, to live differently. Jesus came to model to us what our lives on this earth should be like. He was the epitome of countercultural: He turned His other cheek when His foes beat him; He told us to serve and not to lead; His example was meekness and humility. How many of us are really living righteously? How many of us are living according to the world's standards?

Everything the world stands for Jesus was against. It's no wonder that so many people are living in fear, shame and brokenness. If only we could wake up to the way that our God modeled His life. We must never forget that the first shall be last and the last shall be first in the Kingdom of Heaven. I would encourage you, if you have not done so already, to get in the Word of God! It is like a mirror that God holds up to each and every one of us to show us our true selves. He wants to guide us and teach us through His Holy Word! The Bible refers it as a "lamp unto our feet!" The Word will be a great start to the new life that God has for you!

Trust me, I have tried living for the world. It left me flat broke, alone and fearful of everyday. There were days I woke up wanting to end my life because I thought I had nothing to live for other than the momentary highs and lows of my current situation. At the worst of it all, I found myself in a crummy old apartment reeking of empty beer bottles, marijuana and cigarettes. The floors were a mess and there were beer flies hovering over each trash can. Some of the walls had holes in them from people punching through them in their anger or the fights that would erupt every other night or so. I found myself with a different girl every night and couldn't figure out why I hated my life so much. I was a mess. I had finally hit rock bottom. The irony is my family's world-wide ministry was reaching "coast to coast and around the world" but because of my own poor decisions and disobedience I was literally dying down the street.

One morning I woke up crying out to God for a better life. I heard a tiny, nagging voice inside my head creep up and tell me that I was no good and that I needed to go get a job at the local pizza shop around the corner to supply what I needed to get the next fix or the next 30 pack. I was alone, afraid and hurting so bad but I couldn't show it because my roommates and friends at the time would have made fun of me, telling me to quit being a wuss. I knew God was there but I didn't know how to reach out to Him; I didn't know how to ask for forgiveness.

I was most afraid to turn my life around because I thought that I would have to do life alone. At least with the girls and the beer I had people around me to numb the pain of life. The truth of what my life had become hit me like a ton of bricks, and amidst the sorrow and pain I felt, God's peace came over me like a warm blanket and I felt empowered to let Him help me take hold of my life. That day I told myself no more, no matter what. I had grown tired of the lifestyle I was living and decided to give Jesus a real chance. Immediately, I ended my apartment contract with my room mates (which was really messy) and decided to move back in with my mom until I could get back on my feet. My mom helped me move my stuff out of that apartment in about two hours and off I went into my new life, never once looking back in hopes that God would bring me a group of friends that I could relate to.

A few weeks later I received a call from my grandmother, Jan, asking me to come visit her in Florida and that she had some work for me. Excited about this new adventure, I quickly left to Florida. The first thing I did when I got off the plane was meet her at a friend's house for dinner, a Pastor who she had known for years. When I got there expecting to walk in to a room full of elderly church ladies dressed in their Sunday's best, I was stunned to see a room full of guys my age, who all seemed to be just like me. They dressed like me, talked like me and played sports like me. It was awesome! I thought to myself at first, "I've finally found pastor's kids that like to party like me!"

I ended up staying the entire summer with them hanging out, going fishing, playing sports and connecting through fellowship. After that summer I was going to church with them when it suddenly dawned on me that I had finally found the Christian friends that I had been praying for when I was living in my smelly dumpy apartment back in California. As time went on and I learned more about the Word and what it really meant to be a Christian, I completely turned my life around and gave my life to Jesus. I no longer had to do this Christian walk alone. I had great guy friends who loved Jesus and wanted to be there for me no matter what. They understood what I was going through and who I was and I was never condemned for it. I started to take my walk with Jesus seriously after about six months and decided to give my life to Jesus publicly. Soon after, I began to work full-time with my family for their Christian youth network, JCTV. I was not perfect but I was walking daily with Christ. As time went on, I began to realize that I had nothing to do with my past and that I was completely forgiven and free!

The old was gone and the new had come. Looking back, I realize that I had to push first into God, in order for Him to fully push back into me. The beautiful thing about our Father's love is that He gives us the freedom to choose to love Him, and when we make that choice, He can enter into our hearts completely. Everything I had prayed for while lying in bed, broken-hearted, crying out to God for help, had completely come to pass. It was one of those "be careful what you pray for" kind of moments. The weights that I carried in college and my early twenties had completely dropped off as I began to listen and obey the voice of the Lord.

Push into Him and He WILL push back. That's my prayer for you today. Live boldly for Jesus. Press into Him with your whole spirit, soul, and body. When you admit to Him your true brokenness, when you ask Him to reign in every area of your life, and when you allow Him to mold your desires and dreams to be pleasing to Him, God will transform your life in a way you would have never imagined possible. Brokenness stops at the point where our spirit yields to His will. Don't be ashamed of your past. Ask for forgiveness, and you will be forgiven. Jesus died so that we would not have to wallow in our brokenness and despair, but instead be empowered by His blood and by His love to do great things for His glory! Let the living power of the Holy Spirit inside of you flourish and commit to making each day about living out God's plan and purpose for your life.

The reality still stands that we are human, and we will continue to fail and make mistakes for as long as we shall live- that is just our imperfect sin nature. But if we can change our perspective to recognize trials and tribulations as strengthening exercises from the Lord to help build our spiritual muscle and stamina, we will genuinely be able to count it as joy when we are faced with hard times. James 1:2-4 instructs us to **"Consider it pure joy, my brothers, whenever you face trials of many** kinds, because you know that the testing of your faith develops perseverance. Perseverance must finish its work so that you may be mature and complete, not lacking anything."

The most difficult times I have faced provided the greatest opportunity for complete surrender to God and reliance on His strength, not my own. What a relief it is to know that in spite of my weakness and failures, I have a Father in Heaven who loves me enough to fight on my behalf, to protect me, to guide me, and to mold me into His perfect nature. **I consider it an honor to be broken;** because I know on the other side of brokenness is redemption and wholeness in God's eyes. It is only when we are truly on our hands and knees, admitting to our brokenness that God can fully move in us, to remold us into the people He created us to be. God uses our brokenness to reveal to us our need for Him and to prepare us for future service. Charles Stanley explained it wonderfully by stating, *"Brokenness is God's requirement for maximum usefulness."*

I don't encourage anyone to build their testimony intentionally around being broken, but if you are going through it, remember that He is with you! During the darkest times of my life I can look back and know that God was there with me every step of the way. When I am weak He is strong! Jesus declares to us, "My grace is sufficient for you, for my power is made perfect in weakness (2 Corinthians 12:9)." I count my brokenness as joy and I would not be the same person I am today, blessed beyond measure, had it not been for my past. Moses had his desert, Joseph had his prison, Daniel had his lion's den, David had his cave and Paul had his Arabia. Your story is just as unique and important to God, but before He can bless us, He must break us of our pride, self-will and self-sufficiency. Don't be mistaken to think that God is punishing you, but realize that He is actually loving you into holiness. Brokenness is a heart yielded to God; ready and willing to obey the Holy Spirit whenever and wherever He directs.

Brokenness makes us needy, less legalistic, patient with others, and open to God's purposes. Brokenness makes our hearts available to the Holy Spirit. His one desire for our lives is that we would get back to our original creation. We become a creation that was made in His likeness, Holy and Pure. **Brokenness is actually God's way of restoring us, counseling us and guiding us in his own image.** I pray that God would reveal where you are in the breaking process and confirm what He wants to teach you so that it would be to HIS glory! Where we end is where God begins. He puts the super to our natural. God accepts us just as we are, but he loves us so much, he does not want to leave us as we are.

The greatest story I have ever personally experience about being blessed in brokenness is through the eyes of my grandmother, Jan Crouch. In 2003, my grandmother was diagnosed with a very serious case of colon cancer. By the time the had doctors located it, it had already spread through her entire body and into her lymph nodes; she had lost 3 of the 5 quarts of blood in her system and seemed to be dying by the minute. Her estimated time of survival was only a few short weeks.

Stunned by this devastating news, I remember walking into her hospital room beside my family members who were wailing in sadness and tears, and suddenly feeling an overwhelming sensation of peace and joy. During that time I had been studying Philippians, and the passage from chapter 4, verse 7 immediately came into my mind, "And the peace of God, which passes all understanding, shall keep your hearts and minds through Christ Jesus." As I slowly approached her bedside, taking in the sight of my beloved grandmother who was always so full of light and energy, lying pale and lifeless on a sterile metal bed, strapped into multiple IV's, a supernatural feeling of warmth had covered my whole body as I held her cold, calloused hand.

I vividly remember her asking me to pray with her, and to my surprise, instead of praying for herself or for God to heal her pain she began to pray for others that she knew had the same kind of cancer. I know that if I were in her situation I would have be on my knees praying to God to heal me of MY cancer and MY situation. I don't remember much else and she ended the prayer with an "amen." Later that night, I wrote her a letter describing the powerful feeling of peace and hope that I had when I walked in her room, telling her that God had already healed her and that she still had a big job to do for the Kingdom. I knew from the core of my being that God was going to use her story to touch millions of people that were going through the same thing.

It is with utter praise and glory to God that I can say that in a matter of weeks, God did the miraculous and HEALED HER COMPLETELY OF CANCER! She took no chemotherapy, no radiation. She has been cancer free for over 10 years now. For whatever reason, even being a baby Christian at the time, I had big faith that my grandmother was already healed of her cancer, despite all odds and earthly circumstances that would have lead me to believe her case was hopeless.

I choose to stand upon the words written in the bible that Jesus was pierced for our transgressions, that Jesus was crushed for our iniquities; that the punishment that brought us peace was upon Him, and by His wounds we are healed (Isaiah 53:5). It was then that I fully began to understand the limitless power of our Lord. We often say that we have the faith to move mountains but never really muster up that faith in our own spirits. Our words are usually empty hearted wishes, asking God to do a miracle in our lives, for our own satisfaction and selfish desires.

We don't actually believe that He is going to move mountains on our behalf, much less take care of our momentary challenges. We lack the confidence and faith that it takes to move mountains because it seems too big or we think that God has more important issues to deal with. If God doesn't come through for us in the way that we were expecting, we at least feel justified in attributing it on the fact that we didn't really believe it was going to happen. Let me tell you today, God still heals! He still moves mountains for you and I! He is a good God and loves you so very much! Believe in him and call upon the Lord as you shall be saved, delivered, healed in the Holy precious name of Jesus Christ!

That story alone would leave most in awe and amazement of the power of our mighty God, but it gets better. One evening few years later, now fully healed and stronger than ever before, my grandmother and I began to talk about our walk with God. She reminisced about the letter that I had written in her in the hospital and how she knew that I was in tune with the Holy Spirit when I told her that she still had a big job to do for the kingdom. She was so proud of me that day but went on to teach me a valuable lesson that I will always hold dear to my heart. She reminded me of the intercessory prayer that she exercised while laying on her death bed, and explained that God used the prayers she had for others to heal her of her own cancer. Did you hear that? She explained that God uses our prayers for others to heal the most broken parts of our own lives!

Spiritually, mentally and physically God will heal you of your brokenness when you lay your life down for others. In Matthew 20:16 Jesus says that the first shall be last and the last shall be first. Often that scripture is used to define our leadership roles, but most people don't realize that it is in fact a powerful Kingdom principle to define healing for our own lives! God wants to heal us, but won't allow us to get the glory for all of our own hard work praying for ourselves. We are called to live a higher standard and when we put others before ourselves God does miraculous things! I truly believe that my grandmother was healed because she chose to put others before herself. Regardless of your situation or circumstance, you will see major breakthrough in your brokenness if you continue to seek others well being before yourself. Be proactive about being in fellowship with others who are going through your situation and be intentional about getting on your knees before God on their behalf. Stand in the gap on behalf of their breakthrough and watch God work in a miracle in your own life!

Chapter Twelve

"Down but not Out"

Dr. T.A. Powell – Lynchburg, VA
www.Liberty.edu

T.A. Powell lives with his wife Betty in the Lynchburg, Virginia area where he is a Professor in the School of Religion for Liberty University Online. In addition, he presently serves as the Intentional Interim Pastor for Covenant Community Church of Martinsville, Virginia.

They have one son, Tom, married to Wendy and have four children, Julia, Tré, Jack and Jude. They also have two daughters, Beth, married to David Baxter with two children, Allison and Travis. The youngest daughter, Sharon is married to Casey Downey. They have two girls, Lila and Sophy and T.A and his bride are more in love with the Lord, life and each other like never before.

―――――――――――――――――――――――――――――――――――

MY Journey of Brokenness, Healing and Restoration. Well, there it was. The bomb had dropped, and I sat in a room of the people I loved the most who now trusted me the least. If you told me on that dark, dismal Saturday night that today, my family would be closer than ever, that my wife would not only still be by my side but that our love would be deeper and stronger than I thought possible, that God would use my bad decisions as the foundation of my life's work, I'd tell you, you were crazy.

Let me start at the beginning. During the year, 2003, my life was radically changed. It was a year beginning with outward celebrations but the inward turmoil of my life was reaching a breaking point. There were highs and lows during the course of that year. In February Betty and I celebrated our 25th anniversary of being at the church where I was pastor. In May I finished my Masters Degree at Liberty University and graduated with honors. Many would say we were living a happy fulfilled life. I had a loving, dedicated, faithful wife, three wonderful grown children all married to spouses who served the Lord in our church, precious grandchildren and for the first time in our lives we were enjoying financial freedom.

Still on the inside there was a raging battle of temptation and discouragement. I was dealing with a very divisive staff member in the church who was sowing seeds of discord. By his own admission he hated me with a passion. Clever as he was he never displayed that attitude publicly. I tried frantically to bring some conclusion to our relationship, but he refused. Finally, I mustered up the courage to fire him. He acted with extreme hostility. He left, taking a group of people whom he had quietly influenced. Being careful not to show my hurt I looked happy on the outside but I was extremely distraught on the inside. My feelings were that I had given my life, 25 years to this ministry and it seemed as though God kept saying "no" to me and would not allow it to prosper beyond what I felt it should have.

Those "I don't care anymore" feelings gripped my soul and it was at this time I became even more vulnerable: I let my guard down and Satan blind-sided me. During that time it was the care, concern and sympathy of a secretary that created in me a spiritual vacuum, a compartment, a permission to sin and I did. That which I had feared all of my life and ministry swallowed me. I made the most destructive decision of my entire life. The sinkhole was created and Satan had obtained the victory. I reached the bottom of the slippery slope and fell morally. It seemed like it was all over. For seven months it gnawed at my soul, I was heavy with conviction and I knew that I would reap what I had sown and I was scared to death. I had betrayed my God, my family, my church and my friends and I knew that it was only a matter of time before the end would come.

My daughters had become very suspicious of some of my actions during that seven month period and knew that something was wrong. My wife never had a clue until I admitted it to her on Saturday morning January 3, 2004. Needless to say, she broke down in disbelief and shock. My actions literally tore out her heart, but beyond her broken heart she loved me unconditionally. That Saturday night I called a special deacon's meeting and admitted to them my sin and told them that I was going before the church the next morning and confess to them. They were broken-hearted and many wept openly. They asked me to wait and go before the church on Sunday night rather than Sunday morning. I consented but did not preach on that morning or attend church.

That Saturday night my grown children stayed with me all night long. Of course we did not sleep very much. It was a long, heavy occasion but they constantly assured me of their devotion and love. Then, Sunday night I went to the church, confessed my wrong doing and openly repented of my sin. In the beginning the church embraced us in love and forgiveness. Later it turned to anger and revenge. It was the worst situation of my whole life. I feel the pain even as I reflect back on it now. It is not easy to write about it. I felt that it would have been better if I were dead. I had caused extreme heartache. I was the man who had previously said, "That will never happen to me." But it did.

The next day, Sunday afternoon, before I went before the church, my friend Dr. Johnny Hunt, who pastors the First Baptist Church of Woodstock, Georgia called me and encouraged me to come to Woodstock and rest and in the process to enter the City of Refuge, a ministry of their church which ministers in a professional way, to pastors and full time Christian servants when they have been involved in forced terminations, burnout, immorality and other family issues. I consented and within a week we were in Woodstock. My life, my dreams, my plans were no more. I was a broken world person. I didn't think that I would ever laugh again. The personal pain and the pain that I had caused to those whom I loved the most was almost unbearable. I had become a forced out statistic through my own choices.

My recovery began after Dr. Johnny Hunt invited me to Woodstock, Georgia. Within a week of my public confession and repentance we were in Woodstock and committed our lives in trust to the City of Refuge.

The church provided us a little two bedroom condo located in a rural area of Northwest Atlanta called Waleska. It was situated in a gated community up in the mountains on a golf course forty minutes from the church in Woodstock. My heart was so empty as Tom our son and Sharon our youngest daughter who traveled with us helped us unload the car. We arrived there early on Saturday evening. I remember how responsible and sad I felt for ripping our family apart. Previously, we were living in our dream home with Tom and his family next door, Beth, our older daughter, with her family living behind us and Sharon, our youngest daughter living just a few miles away.

We now were six hundred miles away from kids, grandkids and our familiar, comfortable world. I was broken, lonely, and fearful of what to expect next. I never will forget the tears that flowed down Tom's face as he and Sharon left us there heading back home. Betty and I were there alone, no family, no familiar friends, just us. I could hardly look at her because of the guilt and shame I felt. I had been responsible for literally ripping her heart out and now in desperation we had to pick up all the broken pieces or either call it quits. Everything was so hard to deal with.

Having lost my integrity and credibility trust in me wasn't worth two cents. I wanted to be like the little child who closes his eyes and says, "You can't see me now." I just wanted to hide. It was so painful that a heart attack and death would have been a welcomed event.

We lived in that little condo for a year and a half recovering daily from the greatest adversity of our lives. Each day I would walk up and down the mountainous golf cart paths crying out to God for His mercy and help. Most of the time I put a DVD head set on and played the song with the words, "So breathe in me, I need you now. I never felt so dead within. So breathe in me maybe somehow you could breathe new life in me again. I used to be so sensitive to the light that leads to where you are. Now I've acquired these callouses with the darkness of a cold and jaded heart. So breathe in me I need you now."

Some days as I walked up and down those paths I needed to get my mind temporarily off the situation so I would stray into the woods and pick up lost golf balls. During that year and a half I picked up over 2000 golf balls. Many of them were stamped with corporate images of some of the largest corporations in America. I have them to this day in a golf ball rack in our den. I never gaze at them without thinking of those painful days. At that time I didn't think that I would ever laugh again. A few days after arriving we found ourselves sitting in an office waiting to be introduced to professional Christian counselors who would be responsible for our recovery. I held Betty's hand but felt she was very suspicious of my affection toward her. I felt as though I was a real loser.

During this time I was thinking that the Lord must be really grieved with me. How could I have transgressed in such an awful way? I knew better. However, the Lord showed us His marvelous grace. He loved us. The congregation at First Woodstock loved on us as did Dr. Johnny Hunt, Troy Haas, James Eubanks, Virginia Stephens and Janet Heeter. They loved us unconditionally. We were in a safe environment of grace which quite frankly we had never experienced. We shall forever be grateful. During those ensuing months Betty and I were counseled individually to begin with and later on together. On many occasions we were so exhausted after the counseling sessions we had to go home and take a nap. We were assigned many books to read in addition to the counseling. I did not work during that time. Betty and I were together pretty much 24/7. The church services were so powerful and inspiring at First Woodstock. They allowed me no ministry involvement during that time because among other things I was physically, emotionally and spiritually exhausted. Betty would weep during most of the services which made me very uncomfortable. I later found out that she was weeping for me. She had set her own heartache aside and was feeling so bad that I now had been stripped of what I so loved to do and that was to be a pastor and preach every Sunday. For over 30 years on every Sunday, other than when I was on vacation, I would go to the pulpit and preach God's Word. Now, I would sit while someone else preached. My life and marriage was transformed during those months at Woodstock. Deep down in my life existed habits, fears, problems, attitudes, baggage, and sins that had never been dealt with. I was a time bomb ready to explode and it did. I had carried hurts, injustices, loneliness, and secrets for years. I had no personal accountability to anyone to discuss my hurts and other issues that were in my heart.

As a senior pastor I had no mentor to explain and discuss my feelings of failure and defeats as well as the dangers of success. As a pastor I was

caught up in a performance based, man pleasing co-dependent, legalistic
ministry. I possessed no margin or boundaries in my life. I loved to be
needed and affirmed by men and possessed a great deal of false pride.
I later realized that I loved the ministry so much that it had become an
idol in my life. I loved the ministry more than I loved God. I had never
allowed myself to grieve about anything or to truly get in touch with my
personal feelings. It was through days and weeks of personal counseling
that all of these things became evident in my life and I have been able to
deal with them one by one.

In addition I sat weekly with other men of God who had experienced some of the same sinkholes in life that helped me to become real
and authentic. The dedication of the City of Refuge staff is unbelievable in helping full time Christian servants gain spiritual and emotional
health. Week by week, James Eubanks, my personal counselor, dug deep
into my life and began to pull out all that emotional baggage that I had
carried from a child and during 30 years of ministry. I realized that I
was a product of my nature (Adam) and my nurture (family of origin) as
well as my hidden sins and temptations. My issues were man pleasing,
lack of communication, no authentic accountability, secret unresolved
sins, and failure to deal with conflict, being a controller and trying to
build God's Kingdom for my glory rather than God's glory. We worked
through all of that and I slowly began to see the light of becoming real
and authentic.

After months of counseling, love, grace, provision and a very few
special friends who never gave up on us and loved us unconditionally,
we completed our counseling. When James Eubanks stated in his office
in April 2005 that he believed that we were on the road to a solid restoration we could not help but to give praise to the Lord who knew all
about us from the beginning and no doubt allowed a tragedy to come
so that HE could re-make us into some vessel that could be useable
for His glory. In May 2005, Dr. Johnny Hunt presented to me on a
Sunday morning service at First Baptist Church Woodstock the diploma
of completion from the City of Refuge. Our whole family was present.
A chapter in our life was closing and a new one was beginning.

My feelings are of freedom in Christ, renewed love for my God,
open availability to Him and an eagerness to feel emotions of love, grief,

forgiveness and to experience true humility. My whole family has been affected by this episode in life. My brokenness wasn't mine alone to bear. My wife and my children broke for me and with me, and each of them grieved differently and learned different lessons from this time in our lives. But this isn't world history, written by one victorious person from one perspective. I'll let them tell you themselves how God took the pieces to our lives and put them back together in a more beautiful way than we could have ever imagined.

My Dear Wife, Betty says....

When you love someone with all your heart and have committed your life to him and his dreams in life, when everything you do revolves around him, when he is the one you most want to be with, to talk to share your joys and sorrows with, betrays you....it is nothing short of total devastation to your life. There is no way to really describe the pain that is felt when you have been so blind-sided. My husband of 35 years admitted to having an affair with someone I loved like a part of our family, and my life came to a jolting stop! It was like he kicked me as hard as he could in the deepest pit of my stomach, my legs became numb, my breath was taken away, I felt nauseous, faint and emotionally spent all at the same time. My brain was spinning, was this really happening to my marriage, my sweet family, our legacy? You never forget the day, the place, or the time you receive information you wished you had never heard.

The days that followed were even worse than I could have imagined. That was when the church family heard the shocking news from my husband. I also realized our close knit family was hurt deeply. Everything we had worked for in this church for the last 25 years was gone in an instant. Just a few days later the children, their spouses and grand children and my husband and I are standing in a circle in the yard saying goodbye to each other. We prayed, I don't remember what was said, but I do remember there was a heavy feeling of sadness all around us. T.A. and I were on our way to Atlanta, leaving behind our sweet, but distraught family for the first time in our lives. Two of our children would drive behind us to make sure we arrived safe and sound, then they left us....I will never forget that departure. I felt so alone. The children were left behind to "weather the storm." And it was just that.

The church was so angry with my husband's infidelity that they could not or would not minister to our children. They stayed in the church for a few weeks. All three of them had grown up in this church family, they didn't know where else to go or what else to do with the pain they had. Over the next months, we were loved on by the folks at First Baptist. The grace this church administered to us was a healing balm to our souls. The church we had ministered to, worked and sacrificed for over 25 years had turned their backs on us. They were busy trying to inflict pain on my husband. I realize now; they were hurting also. The church needed someone to come to them and help them through the pain and betrayal they felt, but unfortunately, they did not seek that.

We became full-time counselees in the City Of Refuge program the church offered to us. Three times a week, we would go in for intense counseling. The church paid for our housing and asked us not to work for three months. God so blessed us that we did not work for over a year while there. Life for us was a huge roller coaster as we dealt with all the emotions. This was not an easy effort; it took work and a lot of time. Sometimes, we were so exhausted after counseling, we would have to come home and take a nap. I honestly believe that had we not received the counseling we did, our marriage would not have made it or, had we stayed together without counseling, our marriage would have only existed as cohabitation.

These wonderful folks also brought all our children and their spouses and grandchildren to Atlanta and we had family sessions. They even provided babysitters! The love we felt while there was amazing. Pastors and their families often give and give to a congregation who take and take. This time in Atlanta was a well of refreshment to all of us. Seven years have now passed, and the journey has been an amazing one. I could write a book on what God has done in our lives since those dark, painful days. I can remember when we would go to church, I would feel pain as I knew T.A. was sitting in the pew with me for the first time in our married life, and not in the pulpit where he had been called to serve; the grief we felt when going to see the children in the place we once called home or the uncomfortable feeling of running into someone we knew not knowing how they were going to react to us. But God has healed all of that!

The growth for both of us has been significant, but T.A. has gone through a metamorphosis. He has learned so much about a close relationship with God, about being emotionally healthy and about loving completely. He has taken the foundation he received in Atlanta and added to it a library of wisdom in the books he has applied to his life. We both live in the freedom we know God has given us. We have seen restoration of our marriage and life ministries. We have the joy in our marriage today that only Christ's healing can give. Yes, as you have read, the pain was awful, the betrayal hurtful and the losses were great, but the healing has brought about great peace. I believe deep intimacy with God can only come through trials and sufferings. Brokenness is not a word to fear, because when we are forced to empty ourselves of hurt, pride and control, it is then that we can rely on God to fill us with his love, patience and forgiveness. I knew God had done a work in my heart when I was able to sit in front of the woman who had the affair with my husband, hold her hand, pray with her and forgive her! I could not nor would not have done that on my own. For the first time I truly understood what it meant to trust Christ with my life.

Our family has learned to tap into the inner strength that God enabled in each of us. We have learned much about life, people, love and brokenness. We learned the freedom and power of forgiveness. Forgiveness is a process, not amnesia; it is acceptance, not approval of what has been done. I just want to say, God has blessed us! The blessings came through many tears, but God knew. He had a plan for me and my wonderful husband. I never want to go back to the place I was before He allowed the heartache in my life. I handed Him ashes and He transformed them into beauty.

I have learned the healing power of God's word. I cannot tell you how precious my Bible is to me. While in Woodstock, I would mark certain verses and promises and claim them. There were times then that I would look at those words and hang on by a single thin thread. Today, when I come across one of those marked up passages, I thank God over and over again and there is a sweet peace that comes over me, knowing that my healing has come from His precious word and loving hand. Our family is a true example of what can happen to a life shattered into little pieces and put back together piece by piece by a loving Father. "For I know the plans I have for you, declares the LORD, plans to prosper you and not to harm you, plans to give you hope and a future." And indeed He did!

My Son Tom says....

I was on my way home just days after Christmas with my wife and three small children. We were visiting my in- laws who live in the northern part of the country, about 700 miles away from home. With five hours still to go my sister Beth called me and told me with tears and anger that dad had an affair. I knew this because in September, just four months earlier, I visited my dad at his office in our church where we were all very active. Dad always had an "open door policy." I felt comfortable walking in at anytime and saying hello and joking around with him. This particular time, I felt uneasy because his secretary was coming out of his office and walked right by me without saying anything. That was unusual because we were all very close friends. When I left the office, I returned to my vehicle where my wife and kids were, and I told my wife that my dad is having an affair. She dismissed the idea. I told her what happened, but it still sounded so unbelievable.

I can say that when I heard the news confirmed, I was not shocked. I hung up the phone and told my wife what happened followed by a quick "I told you so." We chatted for a few moments and made comments about how stupid it was, but the remainder of the trip was quiet. This situation separated my entire family. We all lived as close as next door neighbors. We all were very active in church. We hung out some nights, some weekends, and many times during the day. The hardest thing I've ever done is take my mom and dad to Atlanta where they were seeking counseling immediately after the affair was no longer a secret. It was reminiscent of being dropped off for college, except this time I was doing the dropping off. It was only a few short days after the affair was revealed, and while I was dropping them off, I think it finally hit me what was really happening. I was at a place that I was uncertain about how to act or respond. It was the only time I wept for my mom and dad. I wanted them to work through this, and I knew they could. I just felt awful about them having to go through these difficult steps to get to eventual healing. By God's grace healing came and it's still going on.

My immediate family was not as affected because the kids were so young that they did not even know what was going on. It made my wife and me closer, and we vowed transparency in our marriage so that this issue would not creep up on us. At first, we all continued going to the same church. After all, this was my church for 26 years, and at age 33 with a small family, I had built many friendships and relationships that I was comfortable with at my church. It only took about three weeks to realize that continuing to attend the church made it more difficult for my family. We began to feel the blame for what had happened. We left the church, and began to be very complacent about church as a whole.

The only memory of anyone ministering to our hurts was a local pastor, Dr. John Kimball, who invited me and my two sisters along with our spouses to discuss and try to make some sense out of the situation. At that time, it was still too fresh for us to really open up. Although we did not share much with Dr. Kimball, we knew he loved us and we all appreciated his effort to reach out; he was the only one who did. After Dad and Mom left I had to develop my own convictions as an adult, married man. This usually happens at 18 when kids leave home and begin a life of their own. Because I was so close physically to my dad and mom, I never had the opportunity to be a man of my own. I was under their umbrella. I always responded to conviction with "what would dad say" or "how will this affect my dad at church."

It took about 18 months to work out my salvation, but I'm on the winning side. Today, even though my dad lives four hours away, I feel closer to him than ever. Maybe it's email; maybe its cell phone; maybe its text messaging. Who really knows? I'd like to believe that it is because I have a true human respect for him, not as a pastor on a pedestal, but as my dad. I have completely recovered and am a stronger man because of dad's journey of restoration. My faith is stronger. My convictions are stronger and they are my own. My relationship with my current church is stronger. I have no bitter feelings toward anyone, nor do I have un-forgiveness toward anyone who I felt treated us badly and unfairly. I have moved on and life is much better.

My Daughter Beth says....

Sitting in my living room after I had learned about the devastation in our family, I believed I had literally lost everything. Our lives from this day forth would never be the same. We were completely engulfed in the ministry of that church and in that perspective, we truly had lost everything. Outside of the normalcy of my husband, my two children and I, from here on our life as we knew it would change completely. Betrayal was not a feeling that I had from my father-it was the feeling I had from the church ministry. There was no chance at the beginning to deal with the betrayal of my father because of the extreme hurt that came from the people inside the four walls of that ministry. Of course, there were very difficult days, and some days you didn't feel like you could even get out of the bed, but I knew God would not allow this suffering without a great purpose for us. When you have children, everything has to be as normal as possible, so we did the best we could to hide the hurt and pain. I know that our family became stronger through this. Dad was always absorbed by the church and its needs and although he would be at family gatherings, his mind would be on the church and his people. We now have all of dad at family gatherings and functions. His life is still busy, but we really are his first priority now. I began to pray very hard for God to show us what to do and what church to worship and what school for my children to attend. I know this was not God's perfect plan for my dad, but He allowed this to work His perfect plan in my life and the life of my siblings. Seven years later....God is so good!

I have been able to see His plan unfolding and it is so INCREDIBLE. It is far more than I would have ever dreamed that He could do with my family. I look back in my journal occasionally to see what God has done in our lives. Nothing could compare! It took about two years for me to get over the hurt feelings from the people who I felt treated us wrongly. I feel as if I have completely recovered from this chapter in our lives and what an incredible story God has allowed us to have. The future is still yet to be determined. To HIM belongs the glory!

My youngest daughter Sharon says....

So writing this is requiring me to go back seven years, and as weird as it is pretty much seven years to the date. Seeing pain, struggle and dark days in black and white is almost stomach turning. This is my story though, and it is just that – it's mine. Let me set the stage for you a bit. I am the baby of three and grew up as a preacher's kid my whole life. The job was not so bad. I was loved by everyone around me, and had family always around – church family that is. It was as if I had many aunts, uncles, grandpas and grandmas. So the fish bowl living was easy to tolerate since there was such a bond. I purchased my first home that summer and was so excited and preoccupied with the dealings of getting it ready to close and to move in. Everything was going so incredible. I was at the height of my business career with getting a promotion and my social calendar was slammed full. I was deeply involved with mentoring in the summer programs and youth group at church, sang lead in a praise band, sang in the choir, and was playing church softball, with my best friend.

Quickly, my life and the control I had on it began to unravel faster than you can imagine. I began to notice things were not right with my dad. I had noticed some unsettling conversations and looks between him and my mom's best friend, his secretary. I had noticed his family involvement had been tapering off as well. We were his number one so that was extremely weird for me to see. I held these thoughts so very close to myself and would not dare breathe a word of what I thought was ludicrous and frankly felt guilty for even thinking those thoughts.

One October day my sister stopped by my house. I mentioned that I just did not trust anyone anymore. She tried to get me to say exactly what I meant. Was it reality? Was it speculation? Whatever it was, my sister was feeling and had witnessed some of the same things. As I write this I am only feet away from where that conversation took place, and I can still feel the guilt for even discussing it. We decided this would stay between us and us alone! I did not want my mom to find out. My role had always been to be protector and fixer of whatever mom needs. As a pastor, dad was put under a lot of demands and time expectations with other people; I filled his shoes a lot with taking care of mom with making her feel special as she always did with us growing up. So, her not knowing any of this was vitally important.

The next three months were spent following dad's every foot step, phone and phone log, and daily timeline. We took turns following both dad and his secretary, listening to phone calls, tracing their steps. I was determined to prove my thinking was wrong, and that it was my own distorted point of view. I slowly realized it was not creative thinking, but reality that dad was having an affair; that word "affair" and relating it to my dad still makes me feel disconnected from my own body. So, now we were faced with how to stop it with no one finding out, especially mom. It was a question too big for me to wrap my brain around. Surely I can fix this before mom will ever find out and our family will remain together!

Well, I'm sure you can tell now by my writing this account that mom did find out. As the details unfolded, she became such a warrior, a woman I had to let go of to let her be. I thought she would never make it through that kind of news; this is where I first hand witnessed God. At the same time I was first hand witnessing Satan's work in dad. It was an authoritative unveiling of the power of what both good and evil can do when given free reign and influence in a person's life, the powers of the earth colliding-spiritual warfare at its most brutal point. The next step that had to be handled quickly was dealing with informing the church. My brother was in Michigan with his family for Christmas visits. I was desperately awaiting his arrival so he could lead in this devastating situation. Dad met with the deacons and resigned his church; a move I know was so heartbreaking for him. Dad loved God – his family – and the church, but, I believe at this point he was ready to spew it all out and stop the lifestyle he had led for the last six months. We all met back at the house and sat in the living room.

It was so dark and hopeless; mom seemed to take care of all of us, and assured us all something would work out. At that point in my mind I knew they had no jobs, nowhere to go, and would they even remain married? How would our family make it? Would our family survive? I was so angry with dad because for so many years I had tried to stay out of trouble out of respect for his job as a pastor, knowing that if I messed up he would resign his ministry. Yet, he wasn't thinking about us when he made his decisions that he had made recently. He had not been there for me through the heartaches I was experiencing and also in buying my house because he was too busy – too busy taking care of someone else.

My brother arrived that night, and immediately went over to hug dad. Dad was nearly motionless and whimpered in despair. This began the long night before the morning that Dad would face the whole church. I remember this night so well, because it was just us five again – Dad, Mom, Tom, Beth, and myself. There was a silent confusion that filled the room that night. The three of us slept on the floor that night with mom and dad on each couch. The only noise you could hear was the radio playing quietly in the kitchen. We lived in the country and the stations were static at times. The sound seemed to be clear that night as the song "Be near" played several times throughout the night: "for dark is light to You, depths are height to You and far is near but Lord, I need to hear from You – be near, oh God be near, oh God of us Your nearness is to us our good be near, oh God be near, oh God of us Your nearness is to us our good, our good."

As I look back on this night, what seemed to be hopelessness was actually a night I believe God Himself as Comforter was there. He was right there in that living room touching each of us with His loving hands and wiping our tears away as we each needed loving on us each individually as only He knew how to do. The next evening we all met in dad's office. We prayed and formed a bond there stronger than even our bond before. We would walk into the sanctuary together, and we would support each other until the very end. I just knew that the church would rally around us and pray for us and help us through this event. I mean, it seemed likely since dad and mom had always been there for each member of that church through there joys and sorrows. I would soon learn that I was absolutely wrong.

After we had moved our parents to the unbelievable City of Refuge we returned home and in the days and next few weeks to come we would be ignored at church, scorned at grocery stores, gossiped about, and have to attend meetings where the fate of my parents' financial state was being voted on. We finally made a decision between the siblings that our life long church could no longer accept who we were, and that we had to find another place to worship and serve. We then supported each other. All we had ever known was the church people and they were family to us. There were so few that tried to even reach out to us. With my parents moved out of town, and friends all gone, I was in a desperate state. I even went back to church on a Wednesday night and sat in my car and wanted so bad to go in and get some direction and some answers on what I was supposed to do now. I was only greeted with a few members wanting to give me their take on the situation; I guess they figured I had given up on dad like they had, so they were just going to load more trash on him; but he was still my daddy, and that hurt. I was not working now and really had no intention of going back to work.

I never left my house for fear of seeing church people who would turn the other way, and frankly I was an emotional zero after the months leading up to this whole fiasco, and was so dismayed by those reactions around me. It was so tough to deal with betrayal on every angle of interaction in my life. It's like I had been thrust into a different planet of some sort, and I didn't know which way to go, or what to do. I ignored phone calls and cut off all relationships with anyone except for my family and an angel God sent me who is now who I call my husband.

I was in a place I can't really describe in words to you. It's as if the entire world knew the struggles of my family. I visited mom and dad often, but at the end of every trip was returning to my hometown. Dad had done a great job at reaching beyond his church and into the community he was in. So this greatly affected our hometown, and there weren't too many people that did not know in the secular and religious realms; that is just the influence he had. I began to wonder where all the people that said they loved me were at. I was so naive to think that the people of our church loved me for me, and not for my position as the preacher's kid. I felt so lonely. I lived by myself and was doing nothing. I had to drink daily, truly, just to make it through the day mentally. My whole world as I knew it was blown up like an atomic bomb with nothing left to even piece together.

I stopped going to that church and eventually tried out a few more, but it was pointless. I just wanted to be at home alone. The swirl of differences of emotions each day is hard to explain. I wanted so bad to wake up and it all be at the end of this terrible ride. What I didn't realize at the time was each day was needed to experience those feelings. I didn't feel like I could be angry at what was going on because we had to hold our heads high and stick together as a family. Yet I wanted to scream and cut off all ties from any of this. Seven years have passed, and there are not enough words that can give you the highs and lows of the path I have taken. I feel like I am just on the beginning of my journey again with a God that I never truly knew before. My take on the God thing was "do everything you can at church ministry wise, and try to not get into trouble, sing your songs, tithe, and hang out with good people." That's only what people see. The realness of the Christian life comes from the inside, our hearts.

Through this journey I have experienced God, I have not always run to Him, but as I look back on each turn of the events, He was there, in a quiet watchful way. He was there the night the five of us slept in the living room, He was there when I left my parents in Atlanta, and He was there at nights when I was alone and so confused, angry and hopeless. He was there in people placed strategically in our lives years ago that God knew would be our small support team. I now attend a church where freedom in Christ is so apparent. I am always learning new ways how God's qualities of protector, comforter, forgiver, strength, trust, love are worked out in my life. I feel as if even when I worship I understand what I am singing, it's no longer about the words; I feel it. I have been there and experienced His qualities first hand. I worship His character. I look forward to every chance I have to thank Him for His map of my life and newly found freedom. I have seen Him work miracles in each one of my family members. I have seen him make dreams become reality. I have seen Him grow our relationships when I thought before they couldn't get any closer. I thought no family could ever survive this, but we not only survived; we have thrived. I have a daddy now. I never realized how before I had to share him with so many others. It was always my mom I called if I needed anything at all. Conversations could and may have been a bit uncomfortable with dad. I cannot explain to you now how much I have grown to respect my mom and her abilities to guide and to be the glue and warrior for our family, and just how much I have grown to love my dad so very much and grown so very close to him, I am daddy's little girl. My parents' relationship together with God in the center is truly an amazing example to me of perseverance and unconditional love. Because of that I am able to love at a deeper level.

These are my words; this is my heart. I am learning each day how to be a child of God. I have a different view now of God now as a Father.

I am ready to keep growing in His love and to take the hurt, rejected, and hopeless feelings I walked through and see just how much He loves me. I have learned to love others in a real way. My real relationship with Him is just beginning and I am ready to run until I am in His arms of love. He has turned my mourning into dancing; He has turned my sorrow into joy.

The journey continues into the future....

After graduation at the City of Refuge, Dr. Jerry Falwell invited me to come to Lynchburg and join the Liberty University School of Religion Faculty. In July of 2005 I became a part of Liberty and attended Thomas Road Baptist Church. In the fall of 2006 I was invited to start a Sunday school class at Thomas Road Baptist Church. I prayed about it, accepted the challenge and called Troy Haas, director of the City of Refuge, asking him what would he recommend that I teach relating to spiritual and emotional health and he immediately, without hesitating said, TrueFaced. I ordered the study materials that included the life changing, TrueFaced message.

It made such an impact on our class that we decided to turn right around and repeat the whole course again! By God's grace that series of studies helped me to continue my restoration process and made such an impact on me that I could not look at anyone without wondering what kind of emotional baggage might be hindering them from living out of who God says they are. The study consumed me. The three authors of TrueFaced, Bruce McNicol, John Lynch and William Thrall paints a clear distinction between two very different underlying motives Christians sometimes operate under; our determination to please God or to trust Him. TrueFaced shows us how we can trust Him more and live out of our identity in Christ. Most Christians' primary motive is to please God, an admirable motive, but one that leads inevitably to filtering the Scripture through a lens of do's and don'ts, a performance mentality, and an inability to conquer sin, or to be honest about it. People whose primary motive is to please God hide their sin, and wear masks to cover up their own shortcomings. Their duplicity damages their relationships with the people around them and leads to frustration and desperation.

In Scripture, Jesus said they would know Christians by their love, not by their better behavior. The Christian church is paying a high price for its failure to fully grasp the concept of grace. Polls suggest 60 to 80 percent of young people are leaving the church where they were raised, as they see their parents' faith has not worked for them. Turned off by hypocrisy, they seek a place where they can be authentic and vulnerable. The authors tell us that there's a movement afoot now in which people are beginning to say, "How do we create authentic, nurturing environments?" The solution is to make trusting

God the primary motive, not pleasing God. That attitude shift changes everything, as people realize that on their worst day, "God is crazy about them." People fear that if others truly know them, they will reject them, but the opposite is true. Love is a process of meeting needs. If I don't admit I have needs, I never get loved by you. A healthy environment creates a way for me to be safe enough to let you know where I'm failing, where I'm weak. The message of grace is not a license to sin. Grace is the only way that takes sin seriously and allows God's power to deal with sin, not my self-effort, resulting in great openness and freedom. Real grace doesn't take sin lightly. Grace is a soil in which the seed of truth can germinate, and grow this beautiful tree whose fruit is heartfelt obedience.

As a Liberty University professor we are given the privilege to continue our education. As a result of my journey I recently finished my Doctor of Ministry thesis relating it to my personal journey entitled, "Forced Terminations Among Clergy: Causes and Recovery" One of my graduate courses was, The Development of the 21st Century Minister. That course even further helped my understanding of spiritual and emotional health and acquainted me with other resources such as Peter Scazzero's, The Emotionally Healthy Church and Emotionally Healthy Spirituality. We were extensively tested as well as grasping and understanding the journey from our nature and nurture concluding that 80% of the outlook and habits of life come from our family of origin and particularly our Dads.

I think that the understanding of our "Identity in Christ, living out of who God says I am" which I learned from TrueFaced is the key to the Believer's life. When I embraced that truth freedom came to me like

I have never experienced it in my entire Christian life. This journey of restoration has pointed me toward young pastors who struggle in emotional health and churches that are constantly dealing with conflict. I contend that if the local church does not have good spiritual and emotional health then it can hardly have the impact of being a Great Commission church of reaching the world for Jesus Christ. I have recently studied very intensely the role of the transitional pastor with the goal of helping churches in conflict to becoming spiritually healthy. I am presently serving as an intentional interim pastor teaching truefaced principles of spiritual health. Betty and I are trusting God to use us as he sees fit. What has been such a painful journey has turned into freedom, realness and true inner joy.

My passion is to see the church of Jesus Christ get real, authentic, transparent, accountable and therefore heal from all the inside baggage that we have carried throughout our lives. If we could forgive all the sins or wrongs done to us and seek forgiveness of all the wrongs that we have done to others then maybe revival and world evangelization can come before He comes.

Chapter Thirteen

"Beauty for Ashes"

PASTOR MARVIN HARRIS – HUGHESVILLE, MD
www.sm-fellowshipchurch.org

Pastor Marvin Harris and his wife, Dona after losing four children now have three grown children and ten grand-children. Their singles Bible study "Tuesday Night Live" touched thousands of young people over a twenty year span and hundreds of souls were saved, dozens of couples married and scores now into full-time ministry because of their home Bible study and passion for hurting people.

Rev. Marvin Harris is now senior pastor of The Fellowship Church in White Plains, MD and oversees Southern Maryland Christian Academy. To date, they have a thriving ministry and over 100 kids come out weekly on Wednesday night for AWANAS. Had they not lost their first four children most likely they wouldn't been able to touch thousands for God's glory. Marvin and Dona are trophies of grace and love life and the Lord. Dr. Herbert Fitzpatrick, pastor emeritus of Riverdale Baptist Church in Upper Marlboro, MD and Board Member of Liberty University said of Pastor Marvin: "*In my fifty years as a pastor, hands down Marvin Harris is the greatest lay leader I ever had in my ministry. Now that he is in full time ministry as senior pastor I couldn't be more proud of him.*" Frank & Ruth Shelton are members of The Fellowship Church and count Pastor Marvin & Dona as two of their very best friends.

IT'S been 34 years since the tragedy that changed my life, for good. Oh the joy that I have today! God is awesome! He has truly given me beauty for ashes. Growing up, I wanted to go to church, but no one would ever take me. I remember going to my best friends' home at about 7 or 8 years of age. I went on Sunday on purpose because they attended church and I was hoping they would invite me to go with them, but they never did.

In my early teen years I couldn't speak in public. I would stutter or hide. Then I got worldly confidence and started doing the things that the world does. My friend Mike and I would drink together. Many times I would go to his house. His mother Peggy was the only Christian I knew. She loved and prayed and wept for me. One day she got very sick and died shortly thereafter. I went to her funeral and heard the gospel for the first time. I was touched, but not enough to go to church. I introduced myself to the Pastor and got his name, Dr. Herb Fitzpatrick, and left.

In those days my wife Dona and I talked about going to church many times. Finally we made it one Easter Sunday. I don't remember much about the service but I do remember what I prayed that day. I said, "Lord, I don't know what all these people are doing here and I don't know what I am doing here. I have heard the story that you died on the cross and I believe it but I don't understand it. I wish you would show me what it's all about and I am not coming back." I believe God answered that prayer.

From the early age of 6, my dad taught me mechanics. We worked together many years. Although he has been gone for many years now, he is still my hero. I had dreams that someday I would have a boy and we could start a father and son business. My two brothers had girls there were no boys in the family. Our first son Joseph had been born prematurely and died several hours later. Several years later our son David was born. Oh the joy I felt. My dreams coming true! David became the apple of my eye. When he would laugh, we would all laugh.

It wasn't too long that we realized David was having a problem. We took him to Children's Hospital in Washington, D.C. The head of cardiology, Dr. Shapiro, discovered that David's heart was made differently than everybody else's. He had a very rare heart defect, so rare that there was no one to compare it to.

David made medical history every day because his heart only had 3 chambers and only 1 trunk at the bottom. A normal heart has 4 chambers and 2 trunks. Several times we had to take him to the hospital for congestive heart failure. When David was 6 months old we had to take him back to the hospital where they kept him for 24 hours. Back then they didn't allow parents to stay with their children. It was so hard to leave him there.

Early the next morning we went to see him and the nurse told us we had almost lost our son that previous night. My thought was that I may get a few gray hairs over this but that he would be alright. The good guy never looses on television and we were the good guys! Later in the day my wife Dona and I were leaving the hospital to get something to eat. A nurse caught us in the parking lot and told us we needed to go back because David was having trouble. We went back. I went in and looked around the curtain and saw the doctor pumping on my son's chest. They put us in a room and I tried to pray but didn't know how to.

I always felt before that my prayers were always hit and miss. I thought about sin in my life and I felt unclean. I thought no one was listening to me so I prayed my wife's prayers would be answered. After all, she was a good lady! Shortly thereafter, Dr. Shapiro came in and said he was sorry but David was gone. That quickly, it seemed that my hopes and dreams were gone. We went into the room they prepared for us and Dona picked up David and said "Let's take him home. He will be alright." As he turned blue in her arms I thought I would choke on the lump in my throat.

Dr. Shapiro pulled me aside and in our conversation he begged me to let him have his heart. I was trying to be strong but couldn't stand the thought of doing that. David made medical history everyday he was alive. Dr. Shapiro stressed that the research would be used to help future babies born with this defect. Realizing how important this was we agreed. Little did I know that 30 years later Dr. Shapiro and his surgical staff would successfully add a forth chamber to a little boys heart and he lived. Praise be to God. I can't help but think God used David's heart to give life to another, and maybe many more.

In preparing for the funeral for my son, I called that preacher who gave me such peace when my best friend's mother died. He was so nice to us and he graciously consented to do the funeral. At the graveside I knew it was customary to give the preacher a donation. God's word again gave me such peace that I thought I should put everything I had into that envelope. That's how much comfort I had.

Wanting to know more about heaven and needing comfort and encouragement, we decided to go to church. Dona got saved the second time we went and said to me, "You don't have to worry about David anymore. Some day I'll go to be with him!" I thought to myself, what about me, where will I go?

Three months later two men came to our home and shared the gospel with me. In soul winning 101 they tell you if you are there more than 30 minutes you are wasting your time. Those men arrived at 7pm and left at 12 midnight. Why? Because I'm slow and I couldn't believe that God could save me. But he did. Those men thought I had prayed the sinners' prayer to get rid of them. Surprise!

My whole life began to change. Joy and comfort and peace became part of my new life in Christ. We lost three sons and one daughter to this heart disease. We have two girls and an adopted son that are fine. We also have 10 grandchildren that we enjoy very much. I tell people all the time that the death of our children was the hardest thing I have ever been thru but also the greatest! God has given me beauty for ashes. I know one day Dona and I will unite in glory with our children again and there will be some shouting that day. Amen!

What has God done in my life since? We started a weekly singles home bible study. For over fifteen years we averaged over a hundred young men and women. Almost every week we saw souls saved. That is where I met Frank Shelton. He preached his first message at our home. The funny man, Mr. Frank the Impersonator, and his wonderful wife are great encouragers.

At the age of 55, I was ordained to the ministry and took my first church when I was 58. I have been there for 7 years. My motto is "If you don't have a problem, I can't help you." There are hundreds of young people from our ministry and I feel like they are all mine! In my testimony there are 4 things I would like you to remember.

#1 Maybe the child next door would love you to invite them to church.

#2 If you invite people, they will come.

#3 There is no greater blessing than soul winning. Sharing what Christ has done for you. The joy in your heart is indescribable. Once I lead a man to Jesus on his death bed. He told me he was a Sunday school teacher but he was lost.

#4 As an encouragement to those who have lost family or loved ones, I would remind you of Job. He lost his wealth, his health and his children. His wife said, "Curse God and die."

For 38 chapters he looked for the Lord. In Job 23:3 Job said, "Oh that I know where I might find him that I might come even to his seat." In chapters 38 – 42 the Lord speaks to Job and Job says to the Lord in Job 42:3, "These things were too wonderful for me."

Too wonderful? He lost his health, wealth and children. Friends, one day it will all make sense. Take your ashes to the Lord and see if he will transform them into something beautiful!

Chapter Fourteen

"Performance to Peace"

BUDDY MULLINS – SANTA ROSA BEACH, FL
www.BuddyMullins.com

Buddy Mullins grew up in church. Literally! His father was an evangelist and traveled the country to sing Gospel music. At one time it was based more on performance but today its pure and for an audience of One. Buddy was blessed with an amazing gift to communicate through music and he sang with the Grammy Award Winning Gaither Vocal Band and sung in some of the world's largest arenas with legendary Bill Gaither and his homecoming friends. He was best man in Michael English's wedding and sung at crusades with Billy Graham. Buddy's dream came true when he toured with his own group Mullins & Co and Sunday Drive.

Today, he is the Worship Pastor at The Chapel at Crosspoint in beautiful Santa Rosa Beach, Florida. Buddy notes: "God has called me to be a voice to the Church a voice that says let's trust God, and trust in a way that seems outrageous to the world. He is married to his bride, Kari and his greatest accomplishment is being a husband and dad to his two daughters. Buddy while on staff still travels occasionally to sing concerts.

WHEN Frank asked me to be a part of this book, I was honored and yet didn't know exactly what part of my story to write or quite where to start, so I guess I will start at the beginning.

From the time I was born, all I can remember is going to church, playing in church, sleeping through church, getting in trouble talking in church. I guess what I'm saying is our family was very involved in church. With my father being on the church staff and my mother working in the church office, church was a way of life for us.

When I was seven years old my father, Roger Mullins, felt the call into evangelism and a year later, our family joined him traveling on the road from church to church, full time. By that I mean, we sold our house, stored our furniture, and moved into an old school bus where we would live for the next ten years. It was my mom, Cherie, my dad, my sister, Cindy, and me. Saying that I was involved in church is, at this time in my life, truly an understatement because we were literally living on church parking lots for a week at a time as dad would preach revival meetings and our family would sing. I know this sounds incredibly strange to our present church culture, but in the late 1970's this was not such a far stretch for the church. My days were filled with home school and music practice. My nights were filled with dad preaching and our family singing in many different kinds of churches across America. From stiff and stuffy churches, to hallelujah- hollering tent revivals, we saw it all. I loved every thing about our life.

As I was learning and working on music, I truly fell in love with playing and singing. My mom is a song writer and a wonderfully accomplished pianist both classically as well as by ear, but I never had the patience to sit and learn to read notes and follow music on paper. I trained my ear to be as quick as I could at replicating what I heard or being able to sing every part within the chords that were being played. I became passionate about music. Music drove me, and anyone in my family will tell you that to this day, it still does. My father is one of the best communicators I have ever seen, and his ability to truly get a point across either while singing or within his message has impacted me all my life. He made a statement to me while I was a young teenager that I have never forgotten though it has taken me a lifetime to try and accomplish. He said, *"Son, sing great and impress people, and they will remember you for a few weeks, but truly touch them with the message of that song, and it will last a lifetime.* That statement has become my motivation and I still seek to make that my goal today.

As I grew, my passion for performance grew, and I began to really seek to awe people with my talents. As a kid before my voice changed, I would knock the top out singing so high that it would bring people to their feet. Then, when my voice changed, I had to start over and reinvent myself to find that "wow factor" again. This is when I began to pursue communication as the tool. There is nothing wrong with performance, and I believe that it is crucial that we learn and grow, and the teen years are those defining years. I just know that for me, it became my way to gain the attention from people that I craved. I was not always aware of this, but deep inside I loved the power that the platform held and the position that came with it.

When I was seventeen, we were in a "Jubilee" (likened to an indoor tent revival) in Gadsden, AL and a preacher by the name of Jimmy Jackson was giving his testimony on how he was a pastor for some amount of time, and did not even know Christ as his Savior. God spoke to me through him that night. Even though I had grown up hearing the truth and singing about the truth, I finally accepted the truth of Christ into my heart that night. I am grateful to say that my life changed and my mindset changed as well. I began to seek to give God glory through my talents and abilities and focus less on it being all about me.

A few years would pass and though I had grown some as a Christian, I also slipped back into performance mode in many ways with an occasional spiritual wake up call from a sermon or reading the scriptures. But for the most part my pursuit had returned to seeking the glory for myself. When my sister left the road to marry a pastor's son we hired another young man in her place so we could keep singing. Our music ministry continued to grow and within a couple more years, my mom and dad bought a house in Atlanta, GA. I got married to Kerri, and my sister had her first child and mom wanted to be around the grandbaby more, so as she stopped traveling full time and we hired another young man, Paul Lancaster, and then Mark Willett and his brother Wesley Willett, and finally Joel Huggins.

Before we knew it, we were a full-fledge traveling band. Dad was still preaching on Sunday's and we were doing concerts the rest of the week and we were gaining the attention of many in the gospel music world. I had joined mom in writing songs and we were doing a lot of original material and some songs were beginning to travel up the charts. In 1993, my wife Kerri and I moved to Nashville, TN. My father and mother felt the call of God into mission work with orphans in the country of Albania through an organization called Hope for the World. They are still working in that country today and God has used them to make a tremendous difference in that third world country. As for me the move to Nashville never stopped our band, we just adjusted the name from the "Mullins Family" to "Mullins & Co." and kept going. The band kept receiving great press and we were being asked to perform in some of the major venues.

Bill Gaither was one of the men who took notice of our group and began to use us at his "Praise Gathering" in Indiana along with his up and coming "Homecoming" video series. It was during this time that he asked me to become the new lead vocalist for his amazing group the Gaither Vocal Band. For the next two years, I would share my time with my band, Mullins and Co. and the GVB. Things in life were looking good for ole Buddy and I have to admit, I liked being me. Being able to travel with the guys I loved and had traveled with for a few years now and also being able to fly and meet up with the Gaither Vocal Band and do these really incredible events with over fifteen to twenty thousand people every time we would step on the stage. Our band went on tour with Mark Lowry's "Mouth in Motion" tour and then I would fly in to sing with the GVB at the Atlanta Billy Graham crusade. Yea, life was good. I had been climbing the ladder of success, and it sure was warm up there.

In the summer of 1995, Bill decided to make a change in the GVB, and I was back to full time with my band. Though there was some adjusting to do with this change, my focus became a new determination to dig in with these wonderful men that I had been traveling with, and really seek what and where we wanted to head with our music ministry and careers. So, with that we changed our name again from Mullins & Co. to Sunday Drive, and our music took on a much more edgy sound and approach. It caught the attention of a wonderful speaker and author, Josh McDowell who was looking for a new music group to do his latest "Counter the Culture" tour with him.

We did two different legs of this tour from the west coast to the east coast, being truly honored to be a part of such powerful services where thousands of young people came to Christ. This was one of the highlights of my music career. Josh had sat our band down and told us that we were welcome to be a part of things with him for a good long while.

About this time, the music industry began to take notice of our band and we were offered a recording deal from a pretty powerful recording company. The only thing we had to choose to do was to leave the Josh McDowell tour to do a 180 city tour with two other well known artists to secure the deal. After much thought and very little prayer, we decided that the 180 city tour would be best for our career because it came with a major label deal attached. Just another step up the ladder (so I thought).

At the beginning of 1999, we found ourselves past the 180 city tour that did not generate the energy that we had hoped. Our "big" record company had sold out to a "bigger" record company out of New York, and we had been moved laterally within the company which really means "lost in the shuffle." After starting our record deal off with a big tour and our first single going #1, now we were just trying to hold on to each other scratching our heads as to why things had not taken off like we thought they would. The one solace was as a band, we were still all together and we loved one another like brothers. Not far into that year, one of the band members that had been with me the longest, had to make a tough decision to leave the band because we just were not making ends meet and families were at stake. This was a great big blow to me and to the rest of our band, but it was just the beginning of things to come.

As we continued to do the few dates that we had on our calendar, all of the guys in the band had to find extra work outside the group just to make ends meet for their families. Still we continued to plug along out of determination and love, but things were not getting any better. Not once had I thought about calling it quits because we had been playing music together for twelve years now, and we were all like family, and you just music for a youth crusade in N.C.

Since our six member group was now five, I ended up staying in a hotel room all by myself for the entire week. Starting on the first night of that event when I would return back to the room and place my head on the pillow, I would hear the Spirit say to me that it was time to stop and put Sunday Drive in park. That night I just shrugged it off as being tired and a little down about things, but when the same thing happened the next night in the same way, I began to get scared at even entertaining the thought. The third night I started asking God, "okay, if we are suppose to stop this, then what's next?" The room, my spirit, and my heart couldn't have been more quiet.

Therefore, I said to myself that it can't be God speaking because He would always have something else He was ready for me to do. I mean, all my life He had been leading me from glory to glory, just the next step up the ladder, hadn't He? The following night the same message came in the same way and when I asked, what next? Silence. Still God had convinced me that I needed to talk with the rest of the band and call it quits to the dream we had been pursuing. The next morning with a heavy heart, I called the rest of the guys into my room and explained to them what had been going on for the past few nights.

As I spoke, I was noticing there was very little surprise in their reaction and even a couple of them said the Spirit had been telling them the same thing, but they too were scared and afraid to bring it up. Right there in a hotel room in North Carolina, we made the decision to end the dream of Sunday Drive. Through a lot of tears and a time of prayer, we agreed together then set out to finish the remaining dates we had left on our calendar that year. By Thanksgiving, we were officially disbanded and it was truly like a death in the family. I had never experienced depression before in my life, but here it was and it hit me hard.

Here I was sitting at home with nothing to do, nowhere to be, no one calling asking me to come sing. I was sure I heard God say close the band down, but I didn't think He was going to place me on the shelf, but that's exactly how I felt, discarded, shelved, and forgotten. Kerri and I were doing fine in our marriage. We had then three year old Victoria, and Olivia was on her way. My mind, of course began to wonder, how am I going to take care of my family?

Honestly, I never went to college even though I was offered a full scholarship at Liberty University, I turned it down to pursue my music career. I had never learned to do anything else but music and I had poured myself into that all of my life. Now I was 31, a has been in my mind, so what now? I became so depressed that I began to go for counseling with the pastor of our church. I am thankful for Stan Mitchell to this day for being there for this season of my life. I spent a lot of time upset at God during those months, and Stan was right there to listen to me gripe and cry. He would always have the right response and sometimes that was no response at all. My problem I was wrestling with, was that God had always said in His Word that He was our Father and we were His children, but right then, I felt like either He had walked away from me or I had run away from Him. Which ever it was, the relationship was definitely broken in my eyes.

As I desperately tried to keep staying afloat, I would go through bouts of emotion and anxiety attacks. All the while, Kerri was pregnant and going through here array of emotions herself. I truly don't know how she put up with me through it, but I thank God she did. My pastor had suggested I read a book called "Abba's Child" by Brennan Manning. The book was about realizing that you are the beloved of God. I'm not a big reader, so this was a stretch to even get me to start, but I did have a lot of time on my hands so what was going to be my excuse?

As I began to read I came to a chapter all about confronting the "impostor" within. It spoke not just to the false self that we wanted others to see, but most important to the façade that we try to sell to ourselves, believing that this is who we must be to please God, deriving our self worth from other people's observation of us, and then trying to sell ourselves on those distorted images. All the while God, our Creator, who knows everything about us, is telling us we are His beloved and if we could only catch a glimpse of His view of us we would stop trying to measure up to ours or someone else's flawed idea of what gives our life value.

The entire book was great, but there within that chapter is where I began to realize where things were broken in my life. At no fault to anyone else, it was just that I had lived so long in front of people on platforms, television, radio, magazines, tours, etc... that I had lost who I really was in what I do. For far too long I had derived everything about me by this persona that I had become on stage. Now I realize, there are far more talented people than me and ones that have a much larger following, but all of that is irrelevant. It doesn't matter the size of the kingdom as long as you remain king of it, and at this time, mine was in ruins.

I had finally come face to face with my impostor and I did not like dealing with the ugly truth. I asked God to forgive me for usurping His rightful place in my life and made a promise to live honestly before my family, friends, and myself. I longed to restore the broken relationship with God my Father, I wanted to feel his arms around me, hear Him speak, not just read about His presence, but know He was in the room. I remember getting down on my knees one night when my wife and girls were already asleep and asking God to make Himself real to me and help me feel His Fatherly arms of love surround me.

It was at that moment that He took me on a trip in my mind. Like a movie was playing on a big screen, He began to help me relive the night our firstborn baby girl, Victoria, entered into the world. I not only saw everything, but I felt all of the emotions of this miraculous event as if it were for the first time. I remembered as they lifted her up for me to see, I remembered thinking, Oh sweet baby, just breath and daddy will love you and take care of you, keep you safe for the rest of your life. As I was there on my knees tears streaming, God spoke and said, "Buddy, all of these feeling you are having about Victoria, that's how I feel about you." Immediately, the warmth of

His love embraced me as He spoke to my heart and said "It's not what you do, it's who you are, and you are mine, and I love you, and nothing will ever change that." At that moment I realized that nothing my little girl could do would ever lessen my love for her or make it greater.

From her very first breath I already loved her with the full extent of my love and nothing she or anyone else could do would ever change that. God sealed that picture in my heart that night and I realized that I did not have to try to win God's love, or work to keep it, He has given it to me fully and freely. Not based on my performance or lack thereof, but based on His promise. "For God so loved the world that He gave His only son that who ever believes in Him would not perish, but have eternal life."

We are the beloved of God and what a blessed thought in this broken world. I am so thankful to realize what I first thought was God placing me on the shelf and discarding me was truly Him pursuing me and He had to remove all other distractions out of my life so that our relationship would be the only focus I would have. God does not just want the things in our lives that we can't handle, He wants the things we feel most in control of. when we turn loose of the things we think define us and place them in His hands, we then realize who we are created to be. We finally rest in knowing who we are and Whose we are, and we don't have to search for God's acceptance through whatever kind of performance we think we have to do to be accepted by Him. We will then minister out of knowing we have been accepted and loved by Him and the mercy and grace He has bestowed upon us through that love.

The most important stage I will ever perform on in this world is within the four walls of my home as a husband and a father and that's enough. God loves to give good gifts to His children and He has gone overboard in my life. One of the best gifts He has given me was the chance to know Him deeper and closer. Brokenness might be the lyrics, but oh what a blessed melody it has inspired.

Chapter Fifteen

From Grief to The GRAMMY'S

ACTON BOWEN – GADSDEN, AL
www.ActonBowen.com

Acton Bowen is a speaker, NY Times Bestselling author, visionary; many words are put next to his name, but Acton only passion has been to connect people with the living God. Once recognized as one of the nation's leading student pastors, God has blessed Acton with the ability to reach this high tech, attention-lacking culture of Generation Next. In addition to leading xlroads, a city-wide student Bible study in Gadsden, AL, Acton was also was the host of xlroads TV, a worldwide broadcast viewed weekly by millions of teens and adults in every city in America and over 170 countries around the world on network television.

Acton is now a regular guest on Fox News where he serves as a correspondant on Faith and Religion. In his travels, he speaks up to 20 times a month at churches, disciple-now weekends, city-wide crusades, camps, conferences and school assemblies- giving him a live platform before over 250,000 people every year. Acton uses these opportunities and his unique blend of boldness and humor to communicate the life-giving message of the gospel to students and young adults. Acton lives in Alabama where he and his team daily lean into the vision of ABO. For bookings and additional info www.ActonBowen.com

BROKENNESS. In some of us it reminds us of a place. In others it reminds of a person. In many it rehashes an event or series of events. But it rarely ever reminds us of something beautiful. Brokenness is not beautiful. It never is. Most of the time, it's very ugly. But the idea behind this book that you are holding is that there is something beyond brokenness. Truthfully, something is beyond the place, person or event that brought you to your knees. Without question, a place or platform you would NEVER have experienced without the path leading you to being broken.

I guess the first time I ever started to think about the significance of brokenness was, oddly enough, before I had ever been broken. In fact, I was in a groove. At the time, I was blessed to serve on staff at a great mega church, leading one of the fastest growing student ministries in the state. The resume was looking good, and churches all over the country wanted to hire me. Calls from senior pastors were a weekly occurrence, and to be honest, it felt good.

But one afternoon I found myself at The Cheesecake Factory, sitting across the table from a great friend and mentor who knew about all of my accomplishments. I had, and still have, a deep respect for this man. He is not only a dear friend but is one of the greatest evangelists of my generation. I was sharing with him about how I desperately hoped that God was going to expand my horizons and give me a huge platform in ministry. In the middle of my speech, without a warning or lead-in of any kind, he looked at me across the table and asked "Acton, have you ever been broken?" I was somewhat setback. I thought, "What does this have to do with the price of eggs in China?" It didn't seem to fit into our conversation at all! Had he even been listening?

I thought a lot about my answer, but finally said, "No". I was saved at an early age and spent most of my middle and high school years just doing whatever it took to be the fun, funny and popular guy. I wasn't a trouble-maker, but I certainly didn't take my relationship with God very seriously. But then as a senior in High school, I had an awakening. Some great friends came along to challenge me in my walk with Christ, and something real in them began to "click" in me. And my desire to chase after God began to grow. Soon, I was leading Bible studies and small groups at my church. And during my senior year in high school I knew that God was leading me to full-time ministry. My first spot in full-time youth ministry began right out of high school. Every ministry I led grew and every move that I made in ministry "made sense". It was always to the bigger church, with the bigger budget.

So I'm sitting across the table from this mentor who was larger than life to me and I realize that I had never gone through a place of *brokenness*. I asked him, "Why do you ask?" He said, "I asked because brokenness comes when we reach the end of ourselves". I was speechless.

Moments later I got into my car, began my one-hour drive back to my office and prayed a prayer. In my prayer I asked God to give me the strength to go through whatever I needed to face to put me in the place that would bring the most glory I could possibly bring Him. I was scared to death. As I put my seatbelt on leaving the parking lot that day, I also put the seatbelt on preparing for what I knew was going to be a difficult journey...

One month to the day of that lunch meeting, I found myself sitting at the conference room table two doors down from my office in what will go down as one of the worst meetings in history. And that meeting was followed by almost a year of the same. Some things had surfaced concerning a leader in our church and our attempt to deal with it in a biblical manner was being met with anger and resistance. His response was tearing me and four other pastors apart at the core. We sought Godly council, fasted, prayed and asked God to move but it seemed like he was silent. Our efforts to deal with the problem were only met by a resistance and pride that could never be described on the pages of this book- and shouldn't be.

To make a long story short, all four of us knew that we could no longer submit to the authority of this person and we had to resign our positions. The church I had been a part of most of my life, served for 7 years and loved with every fiber of my being was under attack and was splitting... and I felt helpless. How could this be? Why would God sit back and let this happen? Countless hundreds of people who had worshiped and served together for years were now scattered. People felt hurt, confused and disjointed. I was among them. One of the largest and most vibrant churches in the state was now the "talk of the town". The truth was ugly enough and the rumors were even worse. It just didn't seem fair! I felt like God had broken the terms of our "contract". Bad things were not supposed to happen to me! Then, I was reminded of the word "broken"…

The day I was turning in my resignation was quite an emotional day for me. Before I ever left my house I had to call on my dad and several other prayer warriors and friends. I needed strength. I got into my car that day to begin my fifteen minute drive to the office. As I cranked the car I prayed another one of those prayers. "God," I said, "I know I am doing what you are requiring of me, but I need peace. You may not chose to give it to me until I do this, but I would appreciate it now". Putting my car in gear, I wondered if that was even an appropriate prayer as I backed out of my driveway.

Five minutes from my office on a path that I had driven thousands of times, my phone rings. I was still fighting tears and could barely see the number on the screen. Once I could see it I didn't recognize the number. I thought "This is why I have voicemail". But just before I sent the call to voicemail, something deep inside me told me to answer the call; so I did. The voice on the call said in an uncertain tone, "Acton?" I replied with a "yes", and the next five minutes were completely indescribable. The person calling was a ministry hero of mine. We had met very briefly and in passing at a Youth Evangelism Conference in Georgia about two years earlier where he was speaking at the main sessions and I was leading a breakout session for youth pastors. I didn't even know he knew my name, and now he was calling my cell phone.

He told me that he woke up that morning and God had put me on his mind. It was so strong, he added, that as he was running through the airport to catch a flight he literally had to stop what he was doing, get out his laptop, and "google" my name in an attempt to find a way to contact me. That attempt led him to the management agency that was responsible for booking all of my speaking engagements. He contacted my manager, got my personal number and was now at risk of missing his flight to make this call. I was so shocked as I listened to all that he had on his heart. Without a clue about me, my church or anything I had been facing and while running through the Atlanta airport he became the mouthpiece of God to my heart.

He said, "Acton, I called this morning to challenge you in the area of your faith. You may be broken right now, but God always uses broken things." I interrupted him! I couldn't help it. I said "Do you know what I am going through and what I am about to do?" (at this point I was pulling into the parking lot of the church) He said, "No, to be honest apart from hearing about your speaking ministry and travels I know very little about you at all". I began to share with him about my journey over the last several months and we both began to cry. We knew that we were in the middle of a full blown God moment. And the word "brokenness" was back in my mind. My thoughts raced back to that prayer that I prayed over a year earlier in the parking lot of The Cheesecake Factory. I knew that God was setting me up for something amazing. So much so that he was even willing to stop someone in his tracks at the Atlanta airport to give me the news.

That day I resigned. I was still heartbroken, but now with a sense of anticipation and expectation that I had never known; with an excitement that was being birthed out of a year of brokenness. Brokenness led to the end of me. The end of me led to surrender. And surrender was leading me into the wildest journey I would ever take! Walking away from the familiar. Walking away from the paycheck. But walking with the One who had all I needed.

That was almost two years ago now. God was doing something so much greater than I could have ever imagined. He reminds us in His word that he will do "exceedingly and abundantly above all that we could ever ask, think or even imagine". That has been the story of my life.

I was reminded of Elijah. In 1 Kings 17, he has been in the middle of the desert. He was tired and weary and wondering what God was up to. And God led him to a brook. And he miraculously provided food and water for him. But after a while, the brook dried up. Elijah started to dehydrate and started questioning what God was doing. But skipping over to chapter 18, Elijah is on Mt Caramel calling down fire out of heaven and a great revival comes to Israel! See, God didn't take Elijah to the brook to keep him there. God didn't dry up the brook to punish him. He took him there to prepare him for something greater and he dried it up to move him. The brook was not Elijah's source.

My position was not my source. My paycheck was not my source.

My budget was not my source. Jesus Christ was the One who called me by name and prepared me. He was my source! I felt like God was leading me to the end of me. It felt like He led me to the edge of a cliff and said, "Take one more step". Of all the ministry moves that seemed to "make sense" He was now asking me to make the move that made no sense at all. I could have never done it without being broken first.

This last year has been a year of one miracle after another. I have been in 37 states and two countries sharing the Gospel. I have preached live to over a quarter of a million people this year and I have seen over 25,000 repent of their sins and put their trust in Jesus Christ to save them. My ministry has been featured on worldwide television on numerous occasions. I have written books that have landed on the Amazon.com and NY Times best sellers list. I am a regular guest on Fox News where I serve as a Correspondent on Faith and Religion. I have developed relationships and I serve as a spiritual mentor to some of the most influential teenagers in the world through the entertainment industry. I have been commissioned as the Student Evangelism Director for the 2012 Olympic games in London. And this week, I opened my invitation to attend the Grammy Awards in Los Angeles California.

I don't say those things not to say anything about me, but to say so much about an amazing God; A God who is trustworthy with every detail of our lives. In my life it's true. God uses broken things. Think about it! Vance Havner was right: "It takes broken soil to produce a crop, broken clouds to give rain, broken grain to give bread, broken bread to give strength. It is the broken alabaster box that gives forth perfume. We find a broken and bleeding Savior redeeming the lost to Him." And I believe that it's broken people that have reached the end of their abilities, resources, options and selves that will bring the most Glory to the God who is worth of it all. *The brook is not your source.*

Chapter Sixteen

"The Broken Road... to Our Dreams"

MATT BROWN – Minneapolis, MN
www.ThinkE.org

Matt and Michelle Brown are founders of Think Eternity, an evangelistic nonprofit. Matt is the author of *Revolutionaries: Men and Women in Every Century Who Advanced Christianity* and they are frequent bloggers at Thinke.org. Their speaking ministry as international evangelists has taken them to the ends of the earth with thousands of people who have dedicated their lives to Jesus Christ through their ministry. They serve as frequent radio guests, adjunct professors on evangelism, and minister to tens of thousands of people on social media on a near-daily basis.

Recently, Matt worked full time for the Billy Graham Evangelistic Association towards an outreach to the next generation in the United States, held by Franklin Graham, in which 112,798 people attended in four US cities along the Mississippi River. "Matt Brown's powerful messages have been preached from coast to coast across the United States and around the world – impacting large audiences from many denominations. He and his wife, Michelle, represent a new wave of evangelism – communicating the gospel with passion but also with much needed relevancy for a new century. Matt and Michelle Brown are the new faces of American evangelism." -Doug Wead, former White House special assistant to President George Bush & *New York Times* bestselling author. Matt and his bride reside in Minnesota.

WHEN God calls us into His purposes for our lives, many times we have no idea what we are in for. It is so easy to have unrealistic or unhealthy expectations on what it's going to mean to fulfill God's call on our lives. Dietrich Bonhoeffer, a minister in Nazi Germany illuminated this, echoing an eternal truth, "When Christ calls a man, *he bids him come and die.*"

God calls us all to a broken road, but too often believers expect ease and are surprised at their circumstances. Often God gives evident blessings at the beginning of a person's call to give them a glimpse of what He has in store, before taking them into a season of heart testing and preparation. Consider the Apostle Paul, who in Acts 9 experiences the blinding brightness and glory of Jesus Christ on the road to persecute believers in Damascus. This leads to his conversion, and soon he "grew more and more powerful and baffled the Jews living in Damascus by proving that Jesus is the Christ." Within this passage, as is sometimes the case in Scripture, *there are entire years between a single verse.* Paul spends years in the Arabian desert growing in his relationship with Christ, according to his account in Galatians 1:17.

Following early testing, the believer's life is often filled with various trials of many kinds. Paul later passed this truth he had well experienced on to the churches saying "we must go through many hardships to enter the kingdom of God." (Acts 14:22). These hardships break us for our ultimate good. The Psalmist explains, "**It was good for me to be afflicted so that I might learn your decrees.**" (Psalm 119:71). The writer of Hebrews also takes this further: "Do not make light of the Lord's discipline, and do not lose heart when he rebukes you, because the Lord disciplines those he loves, and he punishes everyone he accepts as a son." Endure hardship as discipline; God is treating you as sons. For what son is not disciplined by his father? If you are not disciplined (and everyone undergoes discipline), then you are illegitimate children and not true sons. Moreover, we have all had human fathers who disciplined us and we respected them for it. How much more should we submit to the Father of our spirits and live! Our fathers disciplined us for a little while as they thought best; but God disciplines us for our good, that we may share in His holiness. No discipline seems pleasant at the time, but painful. Later on, however, it produces a harvest of righteousness and peace for those who have been trained by it. (Hebrews 12:5-11).

Both my wife Michelle and I received a clear call from God towards evangelistic ministry when we were still just teenagers, before we ever met. It was amazing when we began dating and fell in love, to find out how God had divinely orchestrated our paths and passions in life.

I was blessed to begin traveling and preaching as an evangelist while still early in my Bible College studies. At that stage, I didn't expect anyone to have me in to preach at their church; my expectations were very low. However, as my wife Michelle and I graduated, tied the knot and attempted to jump into evangelism full time as our living, things quickly became challenging. I already had a few years of speaking behind me and assumed it would get easier, but itinerant ministry can be a roller-coaster of a road to travel. For a time, I experienced emotions of being elated one week and absolutely disheartened the next. Early on, I felt I wanted to quit dozens of times, but didn't know where else to go, or how I could ever quit the calling God had laid so heavily on our hearts.

At several points along our journey I have felt frustrated with God. He was the one who put big dreams within our hearts. We didn't come up with them on our own. I found myself relating to Joseph in Genesis 37 – God gave him dreams that subsequently got him into trouble and eventually being sold by his brothers as a slave. It was God-initiated dreams that caused him this trouble. Of course, in God's great providence this slavery led to him eventually saving many nations of the world. Joseph learned to proclaim: "You intended to harm me, but God intended it for good to accomplish what is now being done, the saving of many lives." (Genesis 50:20).

We see this thread through the Scriptures – *stories of the heroes of faith who's God-given dreams get them in trouble* ... Abraham leads his family from their home to the promised land, arriving to a famine in the land. (Genesis 12:10). Daniel's commitment to holiness and prayer leads him to the lion's den. The list goes on. Over the years of obedience to the call of God on our lives, through various seasons of brokenness, Michelle and I have a deepening understanding of what it means to follow Christ, as He bids us come and die:

Dreams don't always pay the bills

Ministry didn't pay our bills for many years. It helped a bit, but we have worked hard on extra side jobs for years in order to continue in what we felt God calling us to do. The Apostle Paul stated in 2 Corinthians 12:27 that he "often shivered without enough clothes to keep me warm." I'm from Minneapolis, and I understand shivering! Paul, a pillar of the Christian faith, who wrote half the New Testament, and who led hundreds of thousands to Jesus, at times didn't have enough clothes to keep himself warm. He didn't have enough clothes, because he didn't have enough money. Paul knew that the *dreams don't always pay the bills*, and he had the frostbite to prove it. In the middle of his ministry ... not the start ... he had to make tents to even be able to eat. He had the humility and grace to work for his food, and this didn't make him any less of an Apostle. I love what Mother Teresa had to say about this: "Do not concern yourself with your vocation. Concern yourself with your calling, and that is to be lovers of Jesus."

Dreams aren't always full time

Along with not always paying the bills, we experienced as evangelists that it is difficult to keep up a schedule of speaking every week. I remember reading a book about being an evangelist that stated the average full time evangelist couldn't find services 7-9 weeks of the year. That's 3 months. It's easy to see how itinerant ministry requires a life of faith and trust in God and his call.

Last year, I was encouraged to read on one of my favorite blogs by Mark Batterson, a well known author and Pastor in Washington DC, that he hadn't spoken on the road in several months. He probably spoke at the church he pastors, but as far as opportunities on the road, he had a refreshing, needed break. His newest book made it to the *New York Times* bestseller list, he is one of the most read Christian bloggers in the world, and he exhibits incredible discipline in reading hundreds of books a year, and I believe he's only in his thirties. Yet, like the rest of us, God gave him a break too.

Dreams don't always mean security

As followers of Christ, we must keep in mind that the founder and finisher of our faith, Jesus, gave his life for his message. And out of the original twelve Apostles of Christ, and pillars of the Church we preach, nearly all gave their lives in a similar manner – as martyrs for preaching the Gospel boldly around the world. The twelfth, John the Beloved, was supernaturally protected from several such attempts and died an old man. Within our Scriptures are books written from prison by men of God who knew that when God calls us to something he's not guaranteeing ease or security. In fact, it may be just the opposite.

Joan of Arc said: "Everyone gives their life for what they believe. Sometimes people believe in little or nothing and yet they give their life to that little or nothing. One life is all we have, and we live it, and then it's gone. But to give up what you are and to live without belief is more terrible than dying, even more terrible than dying young."

Dreams don't happen overnight

Often people see a person God is using in significant ways and think to themselves – how did they get so lucky? Why did doors open for them? What about me? The truth is that there are no overnight successes. I was deeply impacted reading a book titled *Anonymous* by Alicia Chole. She examines the life of Christ and shows how God wants us to fall in love with obscurity, or whatever season of life we currently find ourselves in. Whatever place we find ourselves in, may we savor the time and freedom we have to study, grow, learn, become, fall in love with Jesus, grow as worshippers, dig our roots down deep, develop our servant's hearts, sacrifice for others to have opportunities we wish we could have and most of all ... learn to trust our God. Dreams don't happen overnight ... but we should be glad they don't. God is too big and has too much in store, and as we follow hard after his heart, he will give us the desires of our hearts at exactly the right time. In hindsight, we will exalt His perfect wisdom and timing.

Dreams don't always end in worldly success

During my regular Bible study, I came across a surprising passage. I had been following the Apostle Paul traveling across great regions of the world bringing the Gospel to the multitudes. I sat in amazement as the Jesus revealed Himself to Saul in a blinding vision on the road to Damascus and the trajectory of Saul's life was completely and utterly transformed. My heart was full as I read of Saul's healing, filling with the Holy Spirit and calling to the Gentiles as Ananias laid hands on him. I followed as Paul moved forward into the beginning stages of all God has prepared for his life since the creation of the world - preaching across great regions of the earth, bringing the Good News of God's sacrifice to many people for the first time in their lives. Over many years, dutifully fulfilling his calling from heaven and seeing great fruit as result.

God led me to this passage ... "Then he ordered the centurion to keep [Paul] in custody, but to treat him with indulgence [giving him some liberty] and not to hinder his friends from ministering to his needs and serving him .. But *when two years had gone by*, Felix was succeeded in office by Porcius Festus; and wishing to gain favor with the Jews, *Felix left Paul still a prisoner in chains*." (Acts 24:24, 27, Amplified). It hit me, *some of God's best people are in chains* ... including thousands of believers around the world today.

The question then begs to be asked: why would God allow this? We know that "the steps of the righteous are ordered by the Lord" (Psalm 37:23) and that the early Church was most likely interceding on Paul's behalf (see Acts 12). But here Paul is after a lifetime of arguably the most pure-hearted service to the Lord of any human that ever has or will live. My initial reaction was that God should ensure that Paul is out there preaching. God had called and gifted him for the proclamation of the Gospel; having already witnessed hundreds of thousands of people personally responding to follow Christ. How many people are missing the Gospel today because of this unholy delay? Now an Apostle and pillar of our Church is sitting and rotting in a jail cell for years on end? We know God's arm is not short to deliver - He had done it before. While there are factors at work that we may never understand on this side of heaven, here are several considerations:

God held him for one: For nearly two years, Paul held regular conversations with the ruler Felix and his wife Drusilla about the truth of Christianity. Many prisoners for the Lord over Church history and around the world today have brought the truth of Christ to the forgotten prisoners of the world. There are times when our ministry is not advancing because God has is strategically placing to bring His Word to one person.

Paul wrote: During Paul's imprisonment in the later years of his life he took time to write to some of his churches around the world. While we don't know if he would have written these "prison epistles" otherwise, we do know his time in prison impacted these letters. We must not miss the multiplication power of writing. Because Paul, sitting in prison, wrote to the Church the message of the Gospel was carried far beyond his actual presence or human capability. Now with scribes copying the Word and carrying it around the world a million times over - these messages are included to this day in the bestselling book of all time - *The Holy Bible.* His writings in those prison cells influencing billions of people across earth today.

God is looking for leaders who are willing to be broken:

11 of 12 of the inner circle of Christ were martyred for their faith. Many other early Church leaders too, including Paul who soon enough was beheaded outside the walls of Rome for his testimony to Jesus Christ. Paul's time in prison and his letters of faith from prison continue to encourage countless billions across earth to stay faithful to the Lord in times of enduring pain and unexplainable circumstance. God doesn't just want to use us to preach - he wants to turn our lives into the sermon.

Dreams are Overrated

Goethe said, "dream no small dreams, for they have no power to stir the hearts of men." While there is some truth in this, Proverbs 19:21 says, "many are the plans in a man's heart, but it is the LORD's purpose that prevails." Any time we are hoping, dreaming and aiming for certain goals in life, there will be a possibility that these dreams will not come true. Or worse, we will grow impatient in our pursuit of our dreams and give up too early. The writer of Proverbs shares this sentiment: "Hope deferred makes the heart sick, but a longing fulfilled is a tree of life." (Proverbs 13:12). Many people across the nations of the earth have experienced the heartsickness of failed goals, unreachable dreams and discouraging days.

We must remember in the pursuit of goals and dreams in this life that we have something greater than dreams. *In His mercy, God breaks us on the path to our dreams – to remove our dependency on things other than the Gospel – for our ultimate good. This enables us to see and savor Jesus Christ above all things, and to place infinite value on His finished work on the cross. In our brokenness we see through our flawed dreams that because Christ went to the cross for us - something greater than our wildest dreams is already done for us.* Because Christ has paved the way and prepared eternity in heaven for us - something greater than our wildest dreams is already waiting for us. All the human dreams we can dream up are overrated when we entrust our past, present and future to Christ. In Christ, we already have it all. It is God-given brokenness that enables us to experience this in its glorious fullness.

Chapter Seventeen

"GET OUT TO GET IN"

FRANK SHELTON, JR – WALDORF, MD
WWW.FRANKSHELTON.COM

Frank Shelton, Jr. loves Jesus and his wife, Ruth and children, Andrew Lincoln & Hannah Grace residing in Southern Maryland. Part author, comedian & visionary but FULL communicator of Biblical Truth, Frank travels the globe pointing people to a personal relationship with **Jesus.** He left the pinnacle of power and corridors of Congress in various Capitol Hill positions "by faith" to preach the Word to the world. He worked for two U.S. Presidents in two White Houses but sole focus is souls and trying to get Jesus elected in the hearts of mankind. Previously, Frank boarded "Air Force One" and flew on "Air Force Two" but content traveling today on Southwest Airlines sharing the Gospel to whomever will listen.

He's an evangelist and encourager speaking over 200 dates per year. He is a frequent contributor on Fox News and has been blessed to appear on world-wide television sharing his testimony of hope and Heaven (TBN, Daystar, Sky Angel, TCT – "Rejoice", "Atlanta Live") and other outlets proclaiming the Gospel to over one million souls annually on radio, television, print and in person. Frank was named a "Distinguished Alumni" from Gardner- Webb University in Boiling Springs, NC and attended the Billy Graham School of Evangelism in Monterey, California. Frank is also the founder of Celebrate Jesus! Crusades based off an assignment God gave him in high school patterned after Billy Graham evangelistic events. Frank is a nationally endorsed spokesperson for Compassion International and a speaker with Upward Sports and has preached twice at Six Flags America for Faith Day. Presently, Frank serves on Advisory Board of Praisefest Ministries "Cruise with a Cause" and together they have witnessed nearly 40,000 come to Christ in five years. Frank also serves on the board of America's Heroes of Freedom raising monies for wounded troops.

Recently, Frank was tapped International Evangelism Chairman for the 2012 Olympics outreach with "Olympian of the Century" Carl Lewis and Lay Witnesses For Christ. He is former VP of National Christian Youth Speakers Network and his radio show "FRANKLY SPEAKING" aired past two years on American Family Radio interviewing weekly some of Christianity's most respected leaders. A fifth generation Washingtonian, Frank's ancestor carried President Abraham Lincoln the night he was assassinated in 1865 across the street from Ford's Theater. Ironically, Frank's father friend was a pallbearer at Elvis Presley's funeral but Frank is reminded daily that he doesn't carry "**The King of a Nation**" or "**The King of Rock n Roll**" but "<u>**The King of all kings**</u>" by his life and lips.

Frank can be found on Facebook & Twitter @FrankSheltonJr
For your next outreach visit <u>www.FrankShelton.com</u>

"**F**RANKLIN, GET OUT!**"** When people call me by my first name it is good. When they call me by my legal name its usually bad. My fourth grade world fell apart. If looks could kill my elementary school music teacher just murdered me. She pointed to the door with intense precision and three decades later I still recall her facial expression. Her face appeared contorted with veins bulging in her neck accompanied by a demonic snarl and it was as if she got a "high" making me feel so low.

I was auditioning for the fourth and fifth grade choir singing

"America the Beautiful" and didn't even finish the chorus when I was cut in front of all my peers and tossed out of class. Literally! To this day, I don't know where that anger inside her came from. She was a volcano waiting to erupt and was the lava vomited out of her classroom. It was not as if I were throwing paper airplanes or painting her walls with crayons while auditioning. Honestly, I did my best and she did the rest! She had in her mind a voice to make up her choir and it was painfully obvious I was not what she was looking (or listening for). Had Bono of U2 been my music teacher I probably gave him the lyrics to his hit song: "I Still Haven't Found What I'm Looking For."

Living just 18 miles from our Nation's Capital even as a kid, I knew that her tact was not the most "politically correct" way to inform a child that they were not needed or "good enough." Today, therapy could have been helpful for that traumatic experience. Most teachers would have created a list informing who made the cut and who got the boot. Others elect to have a private meeting to delicately drop the bomb a day later but somehow I was not only kicked to the curb but literally thrown emotionally through the door. My first reaction was "she's got to be kidding." In elementary school, peer acceptance is everything and as I slowly made my way to the door I was just hoping for the punch line to this horrific joke. However, with my head bowed low and hiding back tears the rescue never came.

From the corner of my eyes as I made my exit I could see the shock on my friends' faces. Bless their hearts they were just as scared as me. We were a team and they also knew that tactic had never been done before in our midst with such harshness to a fellow student. To their credit no one laughed but as my heart was breaking their knees were knocking thinking they could be next. Later on, I learned that others were "cut" but I was the only casualty to be tossed out of class. Hands down, it was the longest day of my young life as I walked back beyond broken to class.

My Dad told me a line from an old John Denver song: *"Some Days are Diamonds and Some Days are Stones."* That day was more than a stone but a boulder and I felt like the weight of the world had just crushed me. I loved "ROCKY" as a child but when you've been hit with rocks (literal or verbal) it isn't fun. What made it worse was not just the sudden shock of being embarrassed before my friends but now walking alone back prematurely to my fourth grade class. By me returning to my seat early without all the other classmates whom auditioned in tow signaled to all as if in neon lights my state and fate. It was as if the word "LOSER" was tattooed on my forehead and embroidered everywhere on my clothes. Some days it would be easier to just disappear and die.

Fast forward a decade and a half and God had called me into the ministry. God had really blessed since that initial rejection (or ejection). In junior high, God allowed me to be the President of the Student Government elected by my peers and I won 701 votes to 99 out of 800 classmates. Even President Ronald Reagan who won 49 states for his second term against Walter Mondale didn't quite have that many percentage votes!

After winning the election in eighth grade I received a letter from Los Angeles inviting me to audition for a leading role in a major motion picture. We were instructed to meet in New York City where kids from all over would try out for this Hollywood movie. Call me crazy but I learned in life that it's nothing wrong with failing but dead wrong to fail to try.

My parents packed the car and at age 13 we headed for the weekend to New York City! I had never felt like such a country farm boy in my life when I saw the larger than life skyscrapers and Empire State Building. The address of that audition was to be on the legendary "Avenue of the Americas." That day we arrived and my parents were informed that they would not be permitted to watch the auditions only producers, casting directors and those trying out. After saying a silent prayer, like Balboa after hearing a bell I came out swinging with my lines and did my very best. I had the strangest calm and felt like I was in a zone. They narrowed the search done and this may sound strange but I believed I 'nailed it." However, in a very pleasant tone I heard from the casting director that I was too tall for the part.

Like cattle we were politely herded out of the ballroom where we auditioned and escorted back to our awaiting chaperones. This rejection was much different. It didn't sting as much and it was an honor to give it a try and do my best. Perhaps because this denial was not as much personal as it was professional. En route on the escalators downstairs to catch up with my parents my mom asked: *"Frankie, how did it go?"* I smiled and with my reply I'm certain she thought I was crazy: "Mom, it went really well. Actually, it was awesome! However, they told me I was "too tall." My mother rolled her eyes thinking I probably lost it and exaggerated and was trying to overcompensate for defeat. Unbeknownst to me as I was sharing my story with my mother in front of me a girl was coming down the escalator behind pointing at me. My mom is now seeing this girl frantically pointing at me while screaming to her mother: "Mom! Mom! That's him (pointing at me). That kid was the best boy to audition in the entire room and he should have got the part for the movie but they told him he was TOO TALL!" Mom, no longer thought that I was "mad in Manhattan." No, I didn't land the role in that movie but it sure felt good to have the vote of one fellow child whom also auditioned.

In high school, it was the best of times and worst of times but God allowed me to play three years on the men's basketball team and crowned Prom King my senior year out of 1,200 students at a public school. By God's grace, I was able to abstain from alcohol, drugs and premarital sex. I honored the Lord and He was now promoting me. Life Lesson: **Demotion comes before Promotion** even in the dictionary.

I graduated from high school in 1990 in my hometown of Waldorf, MD. I wanted to do three things with my life to honor God. I prayed to enter politics, protect the President or preach the Gospel. God allow me to pursue all three vocations while living for Him. After graduating college from Gardner-Webb University in Boiling Springs, NC and working on Capitol Hill, I was also a bi-vocational minister. While working full-time for Congress, I was also on staff as a youth minister at a growing church in Maryland. God was really blessing and I began to realize God was leading me to go deeper in my walk with Him. After six months, I went through my ordination process and only one person was hesitant to ordain me into the Gospel ministry. It was a female who I found out later wanted my job as the youth pastor but she had applied for the position numerous times before my arrival and was never selected. Perhaps she was thinking she would be a "blessing" and try to derail in my life what God was orchestrating. Everyone voted in the affirmative except her. In the words of my dear friend Junior Hill: *"Bless their heart."*

The committee elected to ordain me with once again 90% of the vote (like in junior high) and it was an exciting time. Souls were being saved, lives were touched by God and doors were beginning to open like never before. In August 1998, I was ordained and the sanctuary was packed with family and friends who traveled far and wide to be present. A dozen clergy and church leaders graciously got up one by one and publicly shared testimony of what God had done and was doing in my life. For nearly three hours we praised the Lord and folks kindly expressed their appreciation towards my ministry. My mother said it was one of the most moving and spiritual services she had ever witnessed. Some even told me later that I was blessed because most people in life never get to hear the compliments and kind words that so many showered on me that day. Too often, we wait for a funeral to convey what others mean to us. No question, it was all God.

During the ordination service what made it extra special was when the deacons came up individually to pray a private prayer in my ear while laying hands on me. It was both humbling and honorable and Heaven came down. Words cannot describe or Webster's define what it meant for those gospel giants to speak life into me. In that moving ministry moment what no one else saw or heard the un-imaginable happened. Time stood still when one deacon placed his hands on me while the entire congregation watched but could not hear and what he said next almost knocked me out. He cowardly whispered in my ear: *"Frank, you are in the ministry for all the wrong reasons. You are doing it for a spiritual knot on your belt and I don't see how God could be pleased with you.* Get out while you can." He piously walked off and no one had a clue what just transpired.

It was August 1998, but immediately despite being a grown man (age 26) I felt like I was in fourth grade all over again. His words paralleled my elementary school music teacher and all I could translate was *"Franklin, get out!"* The first experience was for music and now this was in ministry. I saw the face of Satan in the first ejection but I heard the voice of Satan in the second rejection. Immediately, after Jesus was baptized He was tempted by Satan and let out to the wilderness to be tempted and tried. The ink hadn't even dried on my ordination paper and I have a "devout" deacon telling me my ministry was over before it started. It is a fact that cubic zirconia's will always feel threatened by the genuine article.

My heart was broken in elementary school but now my head was ringing from the avalanche of verbal assault as an adult. I had been humiliated in public but now I was just annihilated in private. Its one thing to be hit in the natural but it's another in the spiritual. Truthfully, I couldn't process what was worse. The first cut broke my skin but the second crushed my spirit. Stress and storms are a good time to take an inventory of who is with you. Cancel those whom are against and cling to the One who is for you.

Life goes on and I knew I had to follow the leading of the Lord. Eventually, I took a position at another church and we were quickly becoming the fastest growing church in our state convention. We had a time and once again God was blessing. It was a chance to use my gifts for God's glory and I was promoted from the youth pastor to Minister of Evangelism. The Lord early on had given me a heart for evangelism and with God's leading I began to host youth rallies reaching our county and state. Scores of churches were bringing their youth group to our evangelistic events and God was on the move.

My alma-mater Gardner Webb University had just named me one of ten "1999 Distinguished Alumni" out of the entire 100 year history of all the students to ever graduate. The last two Southern Baptist Convention Presidents, Dr Johnny Hunt and Dr Frank S. Page, respectively are both graduates of Gardner-Webb. It was an honor to say the least. Immediately after that recognition I was awarded a scholarship to attend the Billy Graham School of Evangelism in Monterey, CA. I flew all the way out to the West Coast to attend by myself and was informed out of 900 clergy at the conference that I was the youngest that year to be part of the program. A highlight for me was meeting team members from the Billy Graham Evangelistic Association and getting to hear and finally meet Dr E.V. Hill in person. He signed my Bible and he was a giant in Gospel circles and he died shortly after. Often times when I get up to preach I am reminded of him signing my Bible.

The following year, God opened the door for me to grow as friends with one of America's leading speakers and he was the keynote for two consecutive years with Teen Mania's "Acquire the Fire." He tapped me

Vice President of the National Christian Youth Speakers Network in 2001. Sam Glenn and I co-authored half a dozen books together and he was the "best man" in my wedding. It was an honor to serve the Lord with everything I had and my desire all along was to glorify Him while pointing as many people to Jesus before it was eternally too late for them and my time on Earth up.

Truthfully, things were not right at home and I couldn't put my finger on it but my marriage was a mirage. As a kid, I recall a cartoon where a dam was breaking and this guy was trying desperately to plug his fingers in the gaping holes. Eventually, he ran out of fingers and the dam burst. For months, I was smiling on the outside but dying on the inside but when I said: "I do" to her I vowed "I don't" to anyone else. Married but miserable I was praying desperately that God would fix our marriage but things got worse. My wife began to sleep on the couch and I inquired was anyone else in the picture. I was told "no" but things just didn't add up. For the next few months she avoided church and me. It is hard to be on staff at church and not have your spouse present or support.

On Father's Day weekend in June 2002, I was asked to preach that Sunday service to a packed crowd. It was humiliating to not have my wife and two year old daughter in attendance. My parents drove six hours to hear me preach and spend Father's Day with buy sadly and even embarrassingly my wife wanted nothing to do with me. My mom said later: "*Frankie, I have heard you preach a hundred times but never saw the power of God on you that Father's Day sermon.*" Ironically, when I was at my lowest God was still on High. My world was a wreck, my mind was a war zone and I was crushed that my wife didn't want anything to do with me.

Despite being in a blur I drove home from lunch with my parents after church and absent my wife and child on Father's Day and when I made it to the house I knew something was terribly wrong. My wife met me on the front porch (Father's Day weekend) and said: "*Frank, get out*! I am filing for divorce in the morning!!*" The first time I heard those words it was auditioning for *music*. The second time I heard that statement was the day I was ordained for *ministry* but now those all too familiar words were in regards to my *marriage*. In elementary school, I was thrown out of the class. Today, I was thrown out of my home. Now, I almost threw in the towel.

The rest was a daze. I had been beat before but never blind-sided. Perhaps the reason drunk drivers survive accidents is because they saw the crash coming but the victims don't see it in advance. My first mental reflection resembled a bruised, bloodied and battered boxer dangling on the ropes and I just remember collapsing on the canvas (in my front yard). I had been knocked down before but never been knocked out. The proverbial crowd was screaming but it sounded silent while the Referee was counting and as my world was spinning it appeared as if my wife was smiling. She was determined that we were through and I was out! When I stood to my feet both emotionally exhausted and clearly confused I asked her where I was going to go since I didn't have another plan.

Personally, leaving my family was never an option. She told me that it was my problem – "go figure it out!" She then said with a smirk go stay with your parents!! Actually, a 320 mile trip (RT) wasn't the best commute to work nor in the cards God had ordained for us as a married couple. With my head still ringing and trying to process the news that I had just been delivered what seemed like in slow motion I opened my wallet only to find two one dollar bills. Talk about running on empty I was now on fumes financially and bankrupt of family.

I knew the bridge to my parents was $3 to cross for the toll and yet I didn't even have enough money to get to my mom and dad's house. My wife quickly handed me a $20 dollar bill and told me to leave. Once again my mind processed: "Frank, *get out!*" On Fathers' Day Weekend, I got in my car and as my wife walked into the house with my two year old daughter somehow I drove the longest three hour drive of my life and cried like a baby. Cars are equipped with windshield wipers but God didn't manufacture my eyes to remove tears as I drove on to the next chapter of my life. I had no idea at that moment a book was forthcoming. Honestly, I didn't know if I could even live to turn the page.

The next days, weeks, months and couple years were devastating. In politics and ministry the label *divorce* is not something that is beneficial. I didn't desire it nor deserve it but was dealt it. Questioning God was not something I did. In my heart, I knew He was the Answer. However,

I do recall asking Him on many sleepless nights if He could relate to my pending divorce. In a still, small voice I finally got my answer. He replied almost as if with tears and gently said: "Frank, yes! *I came to my own and my own received me not.*" I had my answer. The Answer, my Redeemer could relate. He had been beaten, battered and broken and even my Redeemer related to rejection (brokenness).

The fact is the most respected are often the most rejected. My wife was engaged shortly after the divorce and my former pastor even asked for his endorsement taken down from my website. Talk about a one-two punch. It was one thing that my marriage was over but now I had a minister who wanted to wash his hands from me too. By God's grace, I was not involved in a sin or scandal in my failed marriage but I was treated the same. Seminary teaches how to handle the woman in adultery but not how to deal with the guy thrown under the bus.

A book needs to be dedicated on how God used my parents, siblings and friends to help during the darkest period of my life. Where a few hurt me many folks ministered to me. For them I say "thanks" but could never repay. God truly used my parents as an extension of His grace and hands to comfort me. Without them, this book would have never been completed. God has a huge reward for them waiting on the other side.

Before the divorce, I shared with my church leadership that I felt like God was calling me to "*do the work of an evangelist.*" I just had finished reading "If You Want to Walk on Water You Have to Get Out of the Boat." The church I was employed was being mightily used of God but I knew that season for me on staff was over. Church was to be a safe haven for sinners to grow as saints but that same lifeline for them was now choking my calling in Christ. The Lord had been dealing with me to trust Him more and step out in faith to share the Word with the world.

While leaving the comfort and secure salary at church many were supportive. In ministry, for me it was never a stepping stone or my intention to build a resume but since childhood I wanted the whole world to know Jesus loved them. The Lord most certainly uses the local church but I had already offers from mega churches to come on staff and quite frankly, even the biggest walls of those buildings were too small. Not in an arrogant analogy but accurate assessment that buildings still have limits and God was calling me to reach the world for Christ as an evangelist. Even 300,000 square foot edifices are small when God called me get on the ball and to *"go ye into all the world and preach the Gospel."* At ten years old, I was the kid who had such a burden for lost friends that I brought 22 kids to Vacation Bible School in 1982. I have yet to meet any other pre-teen do that but I am sure and pray they are out there.

With my decision most were supportive and affirming and for that I will be eternally grateful. Once again, 90% of the church felt we could do no wrong. However, critics are on every corner. Ironically, another deacon from my current church told me after my resignation on my way out the door: *"Frank, you will never make it as an evangelist."* More disappointed than shocked I shared with him in love: "Yes, I will. God has already showed me and ironically, in a few years you guys will probably take credit for what God is going to do in my life." One of my heroes of the faith and friend, Dr Johnny Hunt eloquently said: "If you cannot see it before you can see it than you will never see it." I'm glad God gave me a glimpse of the finish before the start. One great man of God once shared with an apprentice in ministry: *"Son, you will make it if you don't get bitter."*

The deacon to his credit later apologized and wrote the kindest letter asking for forgiveness and even gave a donation to our ministry. It took a big man to admit they missed the ball but that "broken season" was fuel to my fire to focus on what He called me to do. Not to prove others wrong but remind all that Jesus is right and the only way to Heaven. I learned then that we will stand before Christ not critics. In the book of James in the Bible we learn that words are powerful and lately for a guy who had a way with words I had an uncanny way to draw people like a magnet who wanted to cripple me with their callous clichés. It honestly couldn't have got much worse during that dark time for me. The days were long and the nights were longer.

It was so difficult for me to sleep at night during the separation and pending divorce that I considered calling my parents to drive from their home to spend the night with me. One blessing when you are down and almost dead your pride is out the window. I had never felt so defeated in my life. The only thing that gave me comfort at age 30 was placing my

Bible under my pillow at night and me resting on God's Word (literally). It was the only way I could fall asleep when I leaned on God's Word. Plus, my desire to be a good role model for my daughter and longed to lavish love on her is what kept me going.

At times, it was so dark in that single bedroom that I was renting while trying to pick up the broken pieces that I was actually scared. I had heard the phrase before but found out firsthand it was true. The depth of darkness was so vast in my room that one could "cut it with a knife." On two different occasions I woke up in the middle of the night in a soaking sweat only to feel completely sewn to my mattress. It was as if a demonic spirit had oppressed me and embroidered me to the sheets of my bed. My mind was trying to have my fingers and legs move but my body wasn't able to perform the task. Talk about dark days the nights were worse!

Several times while driving home alone (often after preaching) I would have intense impulses from Satan and hear the phrase: "*Frank, hit the gas as hard as you can and run the car into the guardrail.*" It was as if I was paying for the transgressions of another and Satan whispering the all too familiar phrase: "Frank, GET OUT!" It is one thing to be dismissed from choir. Another all together to be disappointed by deacons at church and deeply devastating from my spouse dealt with an unwanted divorce but now Satan was trying to destroy me in death. Regardless, if it were tossed from choir, church or closest companion the devil was clearly tempting me to check out! God really protected me during those trying times and I am firm believer you cannot count out the man whom Satan couldn't knock out.

Trying to breathe after the trauma of divorce was bad enough. It was as if I had been sucker punched and couldn't get air. The second problem was learning to walk again. Honestly, just trying to stand and put one foot in front of the other was nearly impossible. It was like being broadsided in an automobile and instantly enrolled at physical therapy trying to start all over.

Battered. Bruised. Broken. Those three terms portray what I endured in various aspects of my life. A.W. Tozer said: "*God cannot use a man greatly until He has broken Him deeply.*" The Bible records that it pleased God to *bruise* His Son. When the lad loaned his lunch to the Lord and the Father's Son fed five thousand the Bible notes: "He took the bread, gave thanks and BROKE it." Had Jesus never touched it, thanked God for it and twisted (broke) the lad's lunch that meal may have fed a few but never five thousand. The multiplication effect comes only after *being broken*. Picture this – if you never were "broken" you would miss the privilege to minister to the masses.

Charles H. Spurgeon, the prince of preachers also said: "There is a special battalion in the Lord's Army where only *wounded warriors* can serve." Did you see that? Being broken may feel like your enemy today but becomes one of your best friends tomorrow. The Hell you face now is that you can give others Heaven later. Your stifling obstacles initially may place you on God's Special Ops eternally. Your adversity is preparing you for God's Varsity. Henry Ward Beecher penned "Man's best successes come after their disappointments." Hudson Taylor the famed and faithful missionary said "God uses men and women who are weak and feeble enough to lean solely on Him." Oswald Chambers said: "If through a broken heart God can bring His purposes to pass in the world, than thank Him for *breaking* your heart." Elton John sang: "*Don't Go Breaking My Heart*" but Jesus, The Christ believes that part of the breaking leads to the whole of the blessing. Read that again - that line is worthy of a re-tweet!

In February 2011, I preached three times in the pulpit of Dr. Mac Brunson's old church at Green Street Baptist Church in Greensboro, North Carolina. It was an honor to speak for their Spiritual Emphasis Week and at one service nearly 100 students placed their faith in Christ. Dr. Brunson now is senior pastor at the legendary First Baptist Church of Jacksonville, FL and eloquently noted: "*Most of us would like to hear from God while sitting in a Starbucks but the truth is we hear better in a storm.*" William Arthur Ward said: "Adversity causes some men to break; others to break records." Andy Stanley noted: "God may show-case His power on the stage of your weakness." Without question, your mess today may become your message and ministry tomorrow. People relate more to pain than progress and you don't have to be perfect to get promoted by the Lord. Henry Rollins nailed it when he recorded: "Scar tissue is stronger than regular tissue. Realize the strength and move on."

The Bible says: "Happy is the man whom God corrects (chastens).

I like to note "Happy and blessed is the man whom God has broken." Architects when preparing to build massive monuments or skyscrapers often have to dig deep before they can build tall. Your valley is really your victory but just under construction. What felt like devastation was really renovation.

It has been said that the reason your rear view mirror is smaller than your windshield is because where you are going is more important than where you have been. I love that! It is imperative and wise to take an inventory of what God has done for you and where He has delivered you. It is important to have a journal because it is so easy to forget how faithful God has been.

It was an honor to meet Dr Adrian Rogers' wife, Joyce and her interview her on video three years ago in Louisville, Kentucky at the Southern Baptist Convention.

Dr Adrian Rogers was not only a prince of preachers but the king of alliteration. He shared in a sermon once that a blacksmith when making a sword dips it into intense heat. While his masterpiece in the making is in the furnace impurities melt off in the process. The blacksmith in his wisdom knows when it is safe to pull the sword out of the fire. If it stays in too long the heat destroys his work. If it comes out too soon it is not fit for use. Ironically, it is revealed after only one test. **When the blacksmith can see his image on the blade like a mirror finish he knows that it is complete.** Adversity is the ticket to God's Varsity. When false motives, sin and fleshly impurities are removed by the fire of adversity we tend to reflect the image of our Creator like never before. Sunshine may burn you but setbacks will bless you. It takes us going through a refining process to be worth more than gold and begin to resemble God.

Today, I am 39 and turning forty in a matter of weeks. The Lord has been too good to me. The dry seasons are preparing us for a fresh fire and focus around the corner. Those that have endured dry spells get to enjoy serving others fresh food from a buffet prepared by the Bread of Life. Saints whom have been in the darkest dungeon tend to shine the brightest Light when God delivers us. On my radio show I had the pleasure to interview Dove Award Winner Matthew West and he said: "*The broken seasons in our lives brings us out of going through the motions.*" If you want a mediocre ministry than play it safe and act perfect but if you want to be used powerfully for God than let Him have His way with you. Dr Tim Lee's words echo in my ears: "God doesn't do things to us but for us." The Lord is making us even when it feels like we are *breaking*.

This is so crucial so please get this. Being broken doesn't mean we were wrong. It may have transpired because we are living right. Job in the Bible went through Hell. Who needs enemies with "friends" like Job! They kept asking him "what did you do wrong to deserve this?" Here is a word for someone. If you have "friends" who constantly bring up your past than perhaps those friends should become acquaintances in the near future. Forgive them but move forward by faith.

Being broken is not bad. It's a badge of honor to share with the world. You are a victor not a victim. David Ring is right when he says: "I don't have Cerebral Palsy but a platform to talk about God." David Edwards said precisely that God is not your enemy but your friend. We need to grow up and trust God more. If we can trust Him for eternity why do millions doubt Him temporally? All these individuals I mentioned and admire are now on stage. The stage usually comes AFTER the stain, strain and storms. The ultimate goal is not to be on stage but to get off the couch! Walk again and move forward by faith in Christ. If God had a favorite television show it would be *"Father Knows Best."* We have a God who truly desires the best for His kids. If God didn't stop short from giving His very best on the cross why do we think He won't see us through our present crisis? God walks in storms, sleeps in storms and alone can calm storms.

To this day, I still don't know where the violent windstorm came from when I was blown clear out of that classroom but God knew that I needed to experience defeat before I could appreciate victory. Secondly, without humility in the beginning we may be tempted to take the honor away from God at the end. Before we can be catapulted with Christ we need to be chiseled with calamity. **The worse thing is not losing en route to the top but getting there and convinced it was because of our efforts.** "Winning" is not Charlie Sheen's definition but adhering to the plan of God for your life regardless what the score says at halftime. Fortunately, the game isn't over and today you can re-group with God, trust the

Coach and let Him have His way with you and in the end you will not only still be standing but win for all eternity.

President Richard Nixon on the day he left the White House for the last time and as he boarded "Air Force One" in both political and personal defeat said during his last press conference "*You will never appreciate the highest mountain-top until you have been to the lowest valley.*" We can learn much from winners but learn more through those whom lost. Washington Redskin Jeff Bostic played in four Super Bowls winning three with the burgundy and gold before retiring. Ironically, he said that one loss to the Oakland Raiders in 1983 taught him more than the three Super Bowls he won. Be thankful for your seasons of loss.

Today, more than ever I thank God for my setbacks, storms and scars. I used to love God for His success but today I love Him for His scars. His scars proved more than mere words that He loves me. Its one thing to say it but entirely different to demonstrate "while we were yet sinners Christ died for us." I believe the Lord is lovely but also lonely. The Bible notes: "We want the power of His resurrection **but to know Him** is to fellowship in His *sufferings*." Do you really want to know God? Do you really want to go to the next level with the Lord? Do you really want to be used greatly of God? Then you have to change your perspective on being broken.

Willie Jolly says: "*Setbacks are set-ups for comebacks*!" God loves comebacks, second chances and encore performances. It was He alone who came back from the dead in His own strength!! Resurrection is in God's DNA. Yes, it's true I never officially sang in that fourth grade choir. But the blessing is God in His wisdom walked with me through pain not only then but en route to the Promised Land now. Looking back, the Lord was with me each step of the way although I didn't "feel" it in fourth grade. We get hung up on emotion but Jesus hung up on the cross in devotion.

Indeed, for a kid it was a long walk back broken hearted to my classroom feeling dejected and desiring to die. However, His walk to Calvary's cruel cross was far worse. Praise the Lord I was cut as a kid in choir because today, I have been blessed to share the stage with multiple Grammy and Dove Award Winners preaching at various venues along side them as an adult. Yes, I hoped for the school choir but God saw the big picture and that I would later minister with the some of the very best in the world. Sometimes, I smile because God gave me more than the desires of my heart but the dreams of His. Had I got want I wanted I would have missed out on what He had planned all along.

Never let little league critics block your Major League dreams. The one deacon who told me at my ordination that my ministry was false could have derailed me from reaching my destiny with Divinity. Zig Ziglar said: *"More people have gone farther than they could have imagined because someone else believed they could."* Be a builder not a blocker. Over the years, we have all dealt with some "nuts" but it's crucial to stay in the fruit of the Spirit. God has blessed me with some Major League helpers but had to endure some minor league "haters." Sadly, some want you to do well in life but not real well. Truly, sometimes the most respected are most rejected. It is imperative to grasp this lesson of grace – *you will never get ahead with God if you live to get even with others.* Marinate on that for a meal or two.

Dr. David Allbritton is a beloved international evangelist and powerful pastor. He has led literally hundreds of thousands to Jesus and in November 2010, we connected and began to communicate on the phone and online. He has participated in every Olympics as a chaplain with Dr. Sam Mings since 1984 games in Los Angeles, CA. Dr. Mings is the founder of this great ministry and he personally led nine time gold medalist Carl Lewis' father to the Lord on his death bed. Together, they have done a great work for Jesus and Dr Allbritton was telling Dr Mings that I should be part of their upcoming Olympics outreach to London in July 2012. After further review, Dr. Mings graciously named me the International Evangelism Director of the upcoming games with Lay Witnesses For Christ.

A few months later (March 2011), I was flown to Dallas, TX to speak to over 1,300 at the beautiful Dallas-Fort Worth Marriott grand ballroom at the Christian Athlete of the Year Award. Because of Dr. Sam Mings graciousness and Dr. David Allbritton's recommendation they had me sit at the head dais at their black tie dinner honoring Texas finest high school athletes.

Dr. Mings asked me to be one of the two keynotes that night in front of a packed ballroom with "Olympian of the Century" Carl Lewis.

Carl spoke and I was the other speaker slated for the evening. It was not only special but surreal. Ironically, the only thing I could beat Carl Lewis at was running to the buffet line. What an honor it was to be with such giants that evening and God has been way too good to me. After the event, Dr Sam Mings invited me upstairs with his family and it was my honor to ride in an elevator with Dr. Mings and Carl Lewis to the 22nd floor of the Presidential Suite of the hotel and we talked well past midnight about life and the Lord in preparation for this summer's Olympic outreach in London overlooking the gorgeous Dallas skyline. That will be one evening I will not soon forget. Previously, I knew the pain of knowing firsthand being on the outside looking in but it sure was grace to be on the inside looking out. God always has a way to make the crooked straight and the cloudy clear.

After that event in Texas, Dr Ming's ministry "Lay Witnesses For Christ International" ran a wonderful article in Christianity Today and even landed in papers in Australia about my appointment with the Olympic outreach. To God be the glory – great things He hath done. This past summer (2011) Dr. Mings called me to share that Dr Allbritton had developed a brain tumor. Dr Allbritton for the past two decades had served as the International Evangelism Chairman overseeing all the directors and staff of the Olympic Outreach. Sadly, Dr. Allbritton recently died in the Fall of 2011. The man who opened the door for me to go to the Olympics passed away before I could thank him in person and serve Christ alongside him in London. No one could fill his shoes but Dr. Mings asked me to take Dr. Allbritton's slot.

Yes, a deacon (and the devil) at my ordination wanted me out but God and the Olympics outreach invited me in. Your storm today will be sunshine later if you choose to bathe in the Son. **When it rains outside remember He reigns inside** and if God be for you WHO can be against you? To date, God has allowed me to preach the Gospel on world-wide television on Trinity Broadcast Network, JC-TV, Daystar's "Celebration" (twice), "Atlanta Live" three times, TCT – Rejoice, Babbie Mason's show, Family Net (In Touch Ministries) and other outlets. Special thanks to my dear friend, Merry Miller whom God used to open the door for Acton Bowen, Shelley Hendrix and me to be a

Fox News correspondent. I love that quote: *"If you see a turtle on a fence post it didn't get there by accident. It had some help.*" Nearly every other month, it is my privilege to talk about current events related to both politics and religion filming LIVE in New York City, Dallas and their Capitol Hill studios.

The fact is without the occasional hardship as a child I wouldn't be much help as an adult. Life is like a rubber band I am convinced the greater your resistance determines your distance. God has blessed me with a wonderful wife, Ruth and her daddy has been a preacher for 50 years. Ruth had never been married and she didn't see me as someone's trash but a treasure from God. We were married on July 7, 2007. That is 07-07-07 for those taking notes and those are Biblical numbers for restoration, perfection and completeness. God does ALL things well and yes, God is good.

Some suggested that my ministry was over. Dr Johnny Hunt said something that touched my heart: "*Some people messed up and others got messed on.*" Satan viewed me and many of you as an airplane racing down the runway. He thought if he could shoot our tires out before lifting off then we were through but the devil failed to figure out that by God's grace my airplane (ministry) already took off and God delights in broken pieces. Learn to commune with those who celebrate you not tolerate you. At one time, I could barely put one foot in front of the other but I never dreamt that I would walk an aisle again and God would grant a woman who loved me more than her own life. **Religion says you're done but the Redeemer says I just begun.**

One of my favorite stories that I have shared for years is about a young lad from West Virginia. He was walking down Main Street when he passed a barber shop, shoe store and then next in the window caught his eye "Puppies For Sale." The child immediately walked into the pet shop and was in Heaven. He asked the owner: "*Mister, how much for your puppies?*" The owner replied: "Anywhere from $100-$300." The boy dug deep into his pocket and pulled out $1.47. He said: "Mister, I don't even have a dollar and a half but may I at least look at your puppies?" The owner smiled and said "sure."

The owner whistled and out from the back of the store ran four tiny balls of fur. They were the cutest dogs you have ever seen. The boy was thrilled and around the corner to his surprise came another puppy that was limping considerably. The boy's eyes grew as big as saucers and said: "*Mister, what is wrong with that puppy?*" The owner snarled: "He was born without a hip socket." The lad said: "Mister, how much for that puppy?" The man replied: "Kid, you can have him. He is a broken puppy and lame. Why would you even want him?" The boy compassionate grew confident and with a holy anger inside him replied to the owner: "Mister, I only got a $1.47 but in my opinion that "broken puppy" is worth just as much (if not more) than all the other dogs. I want that puppy and I will give you $1.47 today and promise to return every week with my allowance to pay for the balance of that puppy until he is PAID IN FULL!"

The owner in disbelief now nearly shouting at the child said: "Kid, you didn't hear me! The puppy was born without a hip socket and will never run and play like all the other puppies. He ain't worth a dime! Why on earth would you want to pay full price for a broken puppy?" With crocodile tears now streaming down the child's face he didn't say a word but reached down to his Levi jeans and slowly began to pull the cuffs of his pants up only to reveal a broken leg supported by a metal brace since birth. As he wiped his tears from his eyes and his lip quivering he said: "*Mister, I don't run or jump so well either and I bet that puppy needs someone who understands.*"

It is human to long to be understood. It is divine to desire to understand. God's choice candidates of compassion are those whom have endured affliction and still long to serve with a smile. Looking back, I have learned repeatedly in my life that the area that you are initially most embarrassed about becomes your arena to relate and console hurting people. **When God desires to bring hope and healing He doesn't seek Harvard grads for prospects but *broken* people that have been tried and found true under hurtful circumstances to bring a tender touch to those down and out.** When trials come you will either test positive or negative.

In 2005, I was invited to fly to Philadelphia, PA and preach at a weekend Christian singles' retreat. I was scheduled to speak four times in three days in the beautiful hills of the Pocconos. This was exciting, I had never been to this location nor preached to this group and on Friday evening I preached a message I had prepared and God moved. On Saturday, I spoke twice and the Holy Spirit was ministering in our midst. However, between Saturday night and Sunday morning in my quiet time I had a restless spirit and I knew God was dealing with me. That evening, I tossed and turned and God was pressing on my heart to "change my message" for the last sermon.

It is always interesting when God tells you to change course. It was so tempting to preach one of the "old faithful" but I had been learning that delayed obedience is still disobedience. Honestly, I tried to rationale with God during those few hours before my next and last scheduled message with the group. It was clear God was not budging and I would be fudging if I told you I didn't want to do it. The reason was not because I knew better but I was also taught in Scripture to "honor thy father and mother." The fact is, I was still recovering from the recent divorce and my life is an open book. However, my parents to their credit were being protective of me and the last words my mom told me on the phone before boarding the plane to fly to speak to the group in Pennsylvania said: "*Frankie, don't tell them about your divorce.* They don't need to know and some will hold it against you."

God was making it painfully clear through this broken vessel that I had to preach the message He had for them. It wouldn't be easy for me but would ease their pain. You may ask me did God speak in an audible voice? No! It was much louder than that!! In my heart, I was determined to obey God and when I got up to speak it would be completely un-scripted, off the cuff, no notes and speak from the heart. Immediately, I had a flashback in 1992, preaching the sermon that is now the title of this book but had only preached it once. I spoke it then but lived it now "The Blessedness of Brokenness."

Just months before flying to PA to preach I lost a job and it was embarrassing but liberating at the same time and now realized that man's rejection is often God's protection. If that wasn't distressing enough exactly a decade before one of my very best friends committed suicide and I took it personally. Losing someone is painful but not knowing why they died is agonizing. It was now clear what God wanted me to speak to these singles. He wanted me to preach on my divorce, losing a job and the death of one of my best friends to suicide and how God was with me through it all. God gave me my first point with no notes and completely depending on Christ would be "*Appreciating Your Adversities*" (I think even Dr Adrian Rogers would have loved that one).

As the host was introducing me for the last time before I got up to speak doubt crept in and I thought: "What will these Christian singles think if the guy who has been ministering all week now shares that he is in fact divorced? My mind raced, will they stone me or just like old times throw me out of the room. Lord knows, I don't want to offend the host whom invited me to minister. What will they think and I may completely offend or embarrass him and their team? Next, as I share about losing a job in the past what in the world will they think of me now? This "spiritual saint" is really just another "loser" Satan whispered in my spirit tempting me once again to "get out" or worse quit indefinitely. This was certainly going to be interesting sharing for the first time the pain about losing a friend in death to suicide in my sermon. Time for debate was up, I was scheduled to speak. God gave me the order and I had to be obedient.

Then and there, I decided I may go down but at least I will lift Jesus up and honor what He laid on my heart. I said a silent prayer on the front row and as I whispered "amen" the host introduced me, the crowd clapped and as I stood (with no notes) just Jesus and me I began to preach. Partly convinced that this is where I will lose the audience but fully leaning into God's Word and assignment or that moment I preached on. Eventually, I shared about my divorce and you could hear a pin drop. Half way through I heard no animosity but interestingly enough sounds of weeping.

Then I shared about losing a job and how (especially to men) could be disastrous and ironically still no stones were thrown from the gallery. Actually, it seemed the audience was on the edge of their seat and God had them in the palm of His hand. It was evident that God was all over that message and the Holy Spirit was doing a great work and I was a surfer on God's wave just enjoying the ride while pointing them all to the Shore. As I closed my message with losing my dear friend to suicide the crowd lost it and almost the entire room was in tears. To this day, I will never forget what transpired next but God met us on that mountain.

Folks were weeping uncontrollably and they were not judging me but dealing directly with Jesus. God was blessing through a season of my brokenness. I had noticed one woman from the corner of my eye in the second row during my sermon rocking back and forth crying but she really caught my attention when she began screaming "I am healed – I am healed" in the middle of my message. This was not a pentecostal crowd and I was not expecting that. Unbeknownst to me, I was thinking I would offend that packed crowd of 20-50 year old singles when they learned of my unwanted divorce.

The irony is God knew better because over half of them were now single again because they had been through the storm too. That equation had never dawned on me. Sometimes we are so overwhelmed with our situation that we fail to realize that the Savior is still the solution. God uses our good, bag and ugly. When I shared about losing my job I had no clue but three men in the back who reluctantly came to the conference had just got pink slips that week prior to the retreat from their six figure salaried positions and were now un-employed. One of them confessed in private that he was so depressed he contemplated suicide. He had already paid for the retreat but was so tempted to stay home and he gave God one more chance. He told me point blank: "If God didn't speak to me this weekend I was going to check out. I cannot handle losing my job."

God orchestrated that when I finally shared about the pain from my friend's suicide the reason the crowd was weeping was unbeknownst to me two of their members from their church family had also committed suicide in that calendar year and collectively were still grieving and healing from those tragedies. It wasn't pride keeping me from sharing the truth but the price that may come with being so broken. Yes, there is a stigma and a stain from brokenness but a strength that pretending will never have. **Being vulnerable invites God's power.**

That last sermon in Pennsylvania before stepping up to preach I was convinced that I was going to lose the audience. Lose their attention, lose their respect and lose the avenue to minister. However, the exact opposite happened. Ironically, they could relate more to me through my brokenness than my blessedness. Revival broke out and I would have missed it if I preached what I wanted and not what He demanded. Praise the Lord!

As a kid I loved basketball. I played in the sun after school, at recess, in the rain, pitch dark and even in the snow. Over the years, I played in countless local gyms and on several leagues and even coached three seasons while in college. I played on many courts and some of them were banged up with no nets and others were amazing. It was an honor to even play on a NBA court before a Harlem Globetrotters game with legends Meadowlark Lemon and Curly Neal at age 13, when I was in eighth grade.

I will never forget the time I first walked into my junior high school, John Hanson in Waldorf, MD and saw the gym adorned with fiberglass backboards like the pros. I was elated! I felt like I made it "big time" when I saw that beautiful indoor court with glass backboards. What I loved about those professional backboards is that they were transparent. As kids, we called them "see through." As Christians and communicators it is imperative that we are transparent (like those basketball backboards) because truth and sharing our trying times resonate more to help folks not less.

Another element to professional basketball goals is the "break away" rim. When an individual goes to slam dunk a basketball countless goals have been broken because of the strain caused from the force while slamming the ball through the hoop. The break away rim prevents destroying the backboard. If we are ever to see God score in our midst and SLAM DUNK for God we need to "break away" from relying on our own power in the flesh and tap into His strength by faith.

In late 2010, my dear friend Meadowlark Lemon asked me to write the foreword to his new book "Trust Your Next Shot" along with Bill Cosby and Michael Jordan. Over the years, I have found the "greats to be gracious" and Meadowlark is both. It was an honor to meet him in 1985, but two decades later God orchestrated us to reunite and do nearly a dozen events together in several states. Only God could do that! It's always a joy to go from a fan to friend but today, I am still one of his biggest admirers. Meadowlark is known around the globe as the "Clown Prince of Basketball" and inducted into the Basketball Hall of Fame in 2003, and played with the legendary Harlem Globetrotters.

The following year, Christmas came early and I got a surprise call from Meadowlark for me to catch a plane and meet him in St Louis. On December 3, 2011, Meadowlark floored me when he invited me to be his personal guest at his good friend and recent World Series Winner and future baseball Hall of Fame Albert Pujols annual Family Foundation gala in downtown St Louis, MO at the gorgeous Chase Park Hotel.

Albert just signed a $254 million contract with the California Angels the week after our dinner and it was an honor to meet him and his wife along with baseball greats Stan Musial, Lou Brock, Don Mattingly and others while sitting at the banquet with Meadowlark as his personal guest. I had tasted rejection before but it sure was grace to have a seat at the table and dine with my childhood heroes. During dinner, it dawned on me that picture is a snapshot of what Heaven will be like at the "Marriage Supper of the Lamb" — dining with "heroes of the faith" in the presence of the Great One.

Melanie Amaro was a promising contestant in the inaugural season of "X-Factor." She was initially cut by Simon Cowell and was crushed and cried on national television. Simon came to His senses and realized he was wrong for dismissing her and flew half away around the globe to get the girl that he cut. She was afforded a "second chance" and eventually awarded first place by winning the $5 Million purse. She lost initially but Simon chased her, comforted her and crowned her victorious. Melanie being broken in the beginning better positioned her as a champ at the end.

Unlike Simon, Jesus never gave up on us to start. He whom was Divinity became humanity. He was praised by the angels in Heaven but rejected by peasants on Earth. The Lord left Beulah Land and was born in Bethlehem to become the bruised and battered (broken) Lamb to take away the sins of the world. He left Heaven to come to Earth to seek and to save that which was lost. He heals the broken and redeems the rejected. God not only chased us, claimed us but was crucified for us only to crown us as winners with Him.

Brokenness is a blessing. With the rejection in the choir, accusation of my ministry during ordination and cancellation of my marriage to some resembled three strikes and I'm out! In baseball, yes we are out but like Dr. Dan Moore, pastor of Callaway Baptist said **"but in bowling –** ***three strikes and you are on a roll!"*** Humans like baseball but Divinity loves bowling. Jesus hangs out in the "gutter" and uses the foolish to confound (strike out) the wise. Dr. Tony Evans is one of my favorite preachers. I have been blessed to hear him in person several times and met him twice. He has a great gift to paint a picture with words and this incredible illustration is from one of his devotions.

"*A picture of brokenness is that of a wild stallion wanting its independence but being ridden for the first time. It does not want to submit, and it does not want to do what it is told to do. It enjoys a cowboy feeding it, keeping its trough filled with fresh water, and allowing it to go out and nibble grass in the sunshine. The problem comes when the saddle is tossed on its back and the harness is placed over its head. However, if you have watched a horse being broken, you know the cowboy has more sense than to take a new horse that has never been ridden and toss a saddle on its back. For days, the animal may be led around a pen as it adjusts to the pressure of wearing a harness and the conditions surrounding its changing lifestyle. Then the saddle comes out of the tack room and is placed on the horse's back - but without a rider. Finally, the cowboy puts a foot in one of the stirrups. There are many steps in between these, but we can form a mental picture of the process used to break a horse and prepare it to be ridden. When the cowboy climbs into the saddle, the initial shock of having someone on its back is frightening and irritating. The animal begins to buck and rears its head before it begins to settle and trot around its pen. Some horses refuse to be broken and risk being sold. Others, in time and through proper care, are broken and begin the enjoyment of a lifetime of service to their owners. When God begins to work in your life, He doesn't immediately toss a saddle on your back or seek to break you through the circumstances of life. Instead, He works with a plan and goal in mind. Bit-by-bit and inch-by-inch, He brings you to a place where He can train you to live a* life that glorifies Him and is a blessing to others.*"

Only God could take broken vessels and make them beautiful. Praise the Lord that He elects to use imperfect people to promote His perfect Son. Even learning this powerful game changer I realize all too well that life is still uncertain and filled with scrapes, setbacks and occasional storms. Today, being transparent I certainly don't want to paint a picture that everything I touch now turns to gold but its better than that. Much better, I learned to turn everything to God because He is worth far more than gold.

Today, I still have heartache periodically. My ex wife brought my biggest fear to reality in August 2011, when she notified me her work was moving her nine hours away to Dayton, OH and taking my daughter. Visitation every other weekend was tough enough but visits on sparse holidays are horrific. However, part of being broken is learning total surrender. God is watching my daughter even when I can't be present and His Promises remind me that He is a "Father to the father-less."

When I am preaching I believe the reason God has allowed me to give away Heaven so effectively publicly is because of the Hell and hits I have endured in private. Jesus, being broken on the cross enabled our healing and I have found a balm in Gilead. Again, those that have endured the most tend to be used of God the most. Plus, those whom endure now tend to enjoy later. It could be my cross to *bare* but I know I have a God who *cares* and it's my privilege but responsibility to *share.* My daughter, Hannah Grace Shelton is now almost 12 and God blessed Ruth and I with our son, Andrew Lincoln who was born on Inauguration Day, January 20, 2009. As President Obama was coming in our baby was coming out! God has certainly given me double for my trouble and He alone is worthy to be praised.

Richard Bolles wrote an extraordinary piece years ago entitled **"Would You Hire This Man?"** It touched me so much for the last 12 years it has been taped on the inside cover of my Bible.

"A certain church found itself suddenly without a pastor, and a search committee was formed. In due course it received a letter from a man applying for the vacant position. The committee chairman read: "I'm considered to be a good preacher, and I have been a leader in most of the places I have served. I have also done some writing on the side. I am over 50 years old and while my health is not the best, I still get enough work done to please any parish. As for references, I am somewhat handicapped. I have never preached anywhere for more than three years. And most of the churches I have preached in have been small, even though they were located in rather large cities. I had to leave some places because my ministry caused riots and disturbances. Even when I stayed, I didn't get along too well with other religious leaders, which may influence the kind of references these places will supply. I have also been threatened and physically attacked. I have even landed

in jail several times for my preaching. I am not particularly good for keeping records. I have to admit I don't even remember all those whom I have baptized. However, if you can use me, I should be pleased to be considered. I feel sure I can bring some vitality to your church." When the chairman finished reading the letter, the committee members were aghast. How could anyone think that a church of theirs would consider someone who was nothing but a troublemaking, absentminded, ex-jail bird? What was his name? "Well," said the chairman, "the letter is just signed *Paul.*"

A great way to gauge one's usefulness to the Lord is not in their *giftedness* but their *brokenness*. Some scholars believe that the Apostle Paul was also divorced. Personally, it wouldn't surprise me in the least. Regardless, if he were divorced from his spouse Lord knows he was never divorced from his service after "seeing the Light." Indeed, those that have been broken deeply are used greatly.

The late great J.C. Penny was asked if he could summarize in a few sentences the secret to his success. He replied I cannot in a few sentences but will give you the answer in four short words: *"Adversity and Jesus Christ"* is the secret to my success. Life can be lonely at times but God tends to teach us more in our victories than valleys. Tests come in all shapes and sizes. It has been said: "If God takes you to it He will take you through it." God will not only take you *to* and *through* but in the end you'll realize that He is True!

In February 2011, I was invited to fly to New York City to appear as a guest for the first time on Fox News Live. It was exciting and I just finished preaching in Greensboro, North Carolina and caught a plane to LaGuardia. After arriving I was whisked in a beautiful black Lincoln Town Car and arrived at my hotel just three blocks from Times Square in downtown New York City. That evening, I reviewed my notes for the next morning's television taping and tried to get some sleep on the 32nd floor of a gorgeous hotel. It was surreal being back in New York and I had Ruth's support at home but I was on this whirlwind trip alone. Not completely alone, Jesus and me. About three in the morning, I couldn't sleep and I'll admit was nervous. I had done television before but this was a tad different. Immediately, I got on my knees in the dark and next to my bed began to pray. Prayed for clarity, wisdom and that God's love would shine through me on national television.

The next morning, it was pouring down rain and I hailed a cab and took the taxi just four streets. The cab driver stopped, I paid the fare and as I looked at the sign in front of Fox News studios I couldn't help but smile. Despite the rain it was as if God allowed it to dry up the moment I focused on the street sign as my hand was on the door to exit the cab. At first it took my breath away. Déjà vu! The address was 1211 *Avenue of the Americas*. The same street I auditioned 26 years earlier for that role in the major motion picture! God has not only a sense of humor but truly the "author and finisher of our faith." Yes, I was cut as a kid but was back as an adult. God and I both love comebacks!

With a snap to my step, I raced through the rain and it wasn't even an inconvenience. For some it may have been an omen but for me it was "amen!" It was as if while in the

"Big Apple" God downloaded on my personal i-pad as a free bonus a sweet soundtrack that was now playing beautifully on my journey. **When it rains He still reigns.** After checking in, I took the elevator up to their majestic state of the art studios and moments before going "LIVE" once again, I paused and said a brief prayer asking God to use me for His glory. The producer counted down 3-2-1, "we are live" and our host and former Miss America contestant Lauren Green led the way and God showed up.

When the show was over, I thanked the host and shook hands with the other panel and started down the long hallway towards the elevators to head home just Jesus and me with some precious family and friends behind me figuratively not literally. Still processing the excitement of the moment as I was heading out I heard my name and looked over my shoulder and interesting enough the producer of the show was running down the hallway towards me and said "Frank, great job! *We'll definitely be in touch to have you back as a guest in the near future.*" It dawned on me that exactly, three decades before in Maryland as a freckled, fourth grade kid, I was thrown out of class after being cut from my school choir and walked a long, lonely hallway in defeat.

However, on this day as I walked off the set heading toward the elevator of Fox News in New York ironically the producer literally chased me down their hallway inviting me back. It was a sweet moment and once again, I couldn't help but smile. God in His goodness gives us occasional nuggets from Heaven to remind us that He isn't done with us yet on Earth. As I got on the elevator and the door closed I was reminded instantly the words of my father from that old John Denver song: "*Some days are diamonds and some days are stone. Some times the hard times won't leave me alone. Some times the cold winds blow a chill in my bones. Some days are diamonds, some days are stone.*" On that day, in the marketing capital of the world by God's grace it was not a stone but a diamond in the rough. It's been said "pressure is what turns a lump of coal into a diamond." The elevator stopped and as doors opened I walked out to head towards the street corner to catch one more cab to the airport and God gave me another present that the sun was shining, not a cloud in the sky and no trace of rain. Just then the cab pulled up and I jumped in while being whisked to La Guardia for my flight home I saw a street sign "Avenue of Americas" and realized once again that God truly ordains our steps and the words of my buddy, Tony Nolan echoed in my ears: "Go God!"

Delay is never denial. It is clear now that Christ was present each step of the way. Those that have been "broken" and by-passed initially take nothing or no one for granted eternally. Just like Maryland native and world boxing champ Sugar Ray Leonard had Hagler, Hearns and Duran, I had a music teacher, deacons and ex-wife that didn't knock me out but helped prop me up to exalt Jesus more than ever in my life. Today, they are not the enemy but were part of a plan to help me grow as a person and mature as a Christian to be in a better position to be used of God. The Bible notes: "We don't wrestle against flesh and blood but principalities, powers and darkness."

In closing, picture in your mind a hitch-hiker walking down a long road in the hot sun. At one time, he was dehydrated, depressed, defeated and almost dead. He had heard "get out" more than once and a motorist pulls over, rolls down the window and says:

"*FRANK*, GET IN!" The driver was God and I am that hitch-hiker and next He said music to my ears: "I'll lead you Home." Sometimes, we have to hear "get out" from man before we can get in with God.

Remember, it's not who's against you but who is for you matters most. This classic hymn says it all:

"The chime of time rings out the news another day is through. Someone slipped and fell was that someone you? You may have longed for added strength your courage to renew. Do not be disheartened For I bring hope to you. There is no night for in His light You'll never walk alone Always feel at home Wherever you may roam. No evil power can conquer you While God is on your side Just take Him at His promise Don't run away and hide. Chorus: It is no secret what God can do What He's done for others He will do for you. With arms wide open He'll pardon you It is no secret what God can do."

Friend, I got Good News! God is on the look out for the lowly and lonely. He desires to pick up the disabled and races towards the rejected. His specialty is restoring the run down and He lives to bless the broken. God choicest servants are "special" not because they are blessed but because they've been *broken*. Today, I am both. God is not interested in your worthiness but willingness. Satan demands being "worthy" but God just asks are you willing. God isn't interested in your ability or in-ability but availability and only broken people can apply. MEMO: Pharisees, perfectionists and pious punks "get out" but people down and out – "get in!"

Over the years, I had a few suggest along the way that I would never make it but I have a God who told me I would never miss it. The Lord never promised a smooth ride but He guarantees a safe arrival. This book birthed in your hands must now graduate into your head and heart. No more excuses but become an example of God's great grace. Some don't realize until graduating to Heaven that their pain was part of a plan. Strength comes after a strain and the Lord allowed me on Earth to see that indeed we find blessedness in *brokenness*.

Thank you, Jesus.

"But God knows the way that I take; when He has tested me, I will come forth as gold (Job 23:10)."

HOW TO GET TO HEAVEN?

It's as easy as the ABC's

Jesus said: *"I am the way, the truth, and the life: no man cometh unto the Father but by me."* (John 14:6) Good works cannot save you.

"For by grace are ye saved through faith; and that not of yourselves: it is the gift of God: Not of works, lest any man should boast." (Ephesians 2:8-9)

Trust Jesus Christ today! Here's what you must do:

1. Admit you are a sinner.

"For all have sinned, and come short of the glory of God;" (Romans 3:23)

"Wherefore, as by one man sin entered into the world, and death by sin; and so death passed upon all men, for that all have sinned:" (Romans 5:12)

"If we say that we have not sinned, we make him a liar, and his word is not in us." (1 John 1:10)

Be willing to turn from sin (repent).

Jesus said: *"I tell you, Nay: but, except ye repent, ye shall all likewise perish."* (Luke 13:5)

"And the times of this ignorance God winked at; but now commandeth all men every where to repent:" (Acts 17:30)

2. Confess that Jesus Christ died for you, was buried, and rose from the dead.

"For God so loved the world, that he gave his only begotten Son, that whosoever believeth in him should not perish, but have everlasting life." (John 3:16)

"But God commendeth his love toward us, in that, while we were yet sinners. Christ died for us." (Romans 5:8)

"That if thou shalt confess with thy mouth the Lord Jesus, and shalt believe in thine heart that God hath raised him from the dead, thou shalt be saved." (Romans 10:9)

3. Through prayer, invite Jesus into your life to become your personal Saviour.

"For with the heart man believeth unto righteousness; and with the mouth confession is made unto salvation." (Romans 10:10)

"For whosoever shall call upon the name of the Lord shall be saved." (Romans 10:13)

What to pray:
Dear God, I am a sinner and need forgiveness. I believe that Jesus Christ is the Son of God and the only way to Heaven. I believe He shed His precious blood on the cross and died for my sin. I am willing to turn from sin. I now invite Christ to come into my heart and life as my personal Savior. Thank you for saving me and take me to Heaven when I did and use me for your glory now on Earth. In Jesus Name, Amen.

"But as many as received him, to them gave He power to become the sons of God, even to them that believe on his name:" (John 1:12)

"Therefore if any man be in Christ, he is a new creature: old things are passed away; behold, all things are become new." (2 Corinthians 5:17)

WE REJOICE WITH YOU FOR THOSE THAT HAVE TRUSTED CHRIST. Email us Frank@FrankShelton.com to share your decision.

CPSIA information can be obtained
at www.ICGtesting.com
Printed in the USA
FFOW02n1515050214
3421FF